Praise for *The Mary Pages*

"This is a gorgeous, soul-stirring book. There is no sanctimony here—only evocative imagery and poetic prose that lays bare the terrain of a complicated, Mary-haunted, grace-ridden life. *The Mary Pages* is a work of art, an icon in words."

—**Abigail Favale**, author of *The Genesis of Gender* and Professor of the Practice at McGrath Institute for Church Life, University of Notre Dame

"I am in awe at what Sally Read has given us in these pages. What an extraordinary journey she has been on, and she now takes us with her in her discovery—step by patient, even unsettling, step—to understanding the beauty and necessity of falling in love with the Mother of God. There's humor, wit, honesty, vulnerability, poetry (yes!), and a profound understanding of Mary's life entwined with God's, and her radiant presence over the centuries, from Nazareth to Walsingham to Mexico City and a hundred other places. Reader, listen. You will come away changed, even transformed, by what you find in these pages."

—**Paul Mariani**, University Professor of English Emeritus at Boston College

"*The Mary Pages* provides a unique tour through some of the most iconic images of the Blessed Virgin Mary, making them strikingly relevant to women of today. Sally Read's moving memoir recounts the dilemmas and distractions of modern women, but also reveals her poignant game of hide-and-seek with the Mother of God through a series of works of art. As a poet who searches for meaning beyond the immediate, Sally Read helps the reader see that those faces of Mary—above altars, in museums, by bedsides—are calling to her children in whatever circumstances they may find themselves. A truly inspiring read."

—**Elizabeth Lev**, art historian and author of *How Catholic Art Saved the Faith*

"'If anyone is in Christ,' writes St. Paul to the Corinthians, 'he is a new creation.' Through her search for some real Mary represented in art, Read examines her own life as a self-creation, seeking 'liberation' in a fallen and sordid world. What Mary, the 'unsurpassed solely human icon,' reveals to her is that her 'body was made to be a piece of Eden.' It is in recognizing in the Blessed Mother an image of what it is to be a 'new creation' that the writer finds her own soul luminously remade."

—**Sally Thomas**, author of *Works of Mercy*

"Sally Read follows a winding path into the Church, led by the arresting beauty of Mary's fiat, not a sanded-off, sentimental, safe kind of love. Read's own prose mirrors the jarring loveliness of God's invitation."

—**Leah Libresco Sargeant**, author of *Arriving at Amen: Seven Catholic Prayers That Even I Can Offer*

The
Mary
Pages

The Mary Pages

AN ATHEIST'S JOURNEY TO THE MOTHER OF GOD

SALLY READ

Published by Word on Fire, Elk Grove Village, IL 60007
© 2024 by Sally Read
Printed in the United States of America
All rights reserved

Cover design by Rozann Lee, typesetting by Marlene Burrell, and
interior art direction by Nicolas Fredrickson and Rozann Lee

Scripture excerpts are from the New Revised Standard Version Bible:
Catholic Edition (copyright © 1989, 1993), used by permission of the
National Council of the Churches of Christ in the United States of America.
All rights reserved worldwide.

Excerpt from the English translation of the *Catechism of the Catholic Church*
for use in the United States of America copyright © 1994, United States
Catholic Conference, Inc.—Libreria Editrice Vaticana. Used by permission.
English translation of the *Catechism of the Catholic Church*: Modifications
from the Editio Typica copyright © 1997, United States Conference of
Catholic Bishops—Libreria Editrice Vaticana.

ISBN: 978-1-68578-113-2

Library of Congress Control Number: 2024938895

For Sofia Abasolo
And, of course, for Mary

Wild air, world-mothering air

—Gerard Manley Hopkins

I love all things that need my lover's life,
And live to give my newborn Morning to your quiet rooms

—Thomas Merton

Tell all the Truth but tell it slant—
Success in Circuit lies
Too bright for our infirm Delight
The Truth's superb surprise
As Lightning to the Children eased
With explanation kind
The Truth must dazzle gradually
Or every man be blind—

—Emily Dickinson

Contents

Acknowledgments

Thank you to all of those who kept the faith with this book and encouraged me along the way, particularly my uncle Kerry Lee Crabbe, who was so enthusiastic about my Mary writing, but very sadly did not live to see the publication of *The Mary Pages*.

And thank you to the design and editorial teams at Word on Fire for letting the story reach those who are curious about Mary and those who simply love her.

A Note to the Reader

This is a literary memoir, combined at times with what might be termed historical fiction. Let me explain how I have worked within both those genres.

With regard to literary memoir, all the personal stories told here are true. Please bear in mind, however, that I have sometimes changed details to protect the privacy of the real people involved. As such, I've occasionally dispensed with a documentary respect for real names and locations. The *literary* aspect of literary memoir means that I have favored the shaping of narrative over what would otherwise be a succession of diary entries. These narrative choices (the way in which we tell a tale: where we begin and end, what we leave out or include, and how we order the telling of events) are about finding the best way to illuminate the action of Mary in my life. Readers of my 2016 memoir *Night's Bright Darkness* will recognize here a limited number of events that were told in a briefer or more peripheral way in that book. *The Mary Pages* casts new light on those events and takes both reader and writer into previously unnavigated territory.

As far as historical fiction goes, I believe John Donne's assertion that no man is an island. That is to say, Mary's role in others' lives also impacts my own life. I have therefore, very occasionally, interwoven narratives from what we know of decades- or centuries-old happenings with my story. In doing so, I hope I have uncovered Mary's role in those distant events—or how God, through Mary, has used those events to reach me. Instead of historical fiction, we might call these sections "Marian Narrative": they involve looking at stories with an eye for her vigilant presence.

La Madonna del Granduca
by Raphael, 1506–1507

My First Marys

I first saw her in my grandparents' house—a luminous oval in the darkness of an oil painting. I'd lie on the settee in the afternoons, with nothing before me but climbing on haybales and soft-boiled eggs for tea, and look at her. I didn't marvel at how her skin glowed like olive oil (I didn't know olive oil). I couldn't have begun to consider the genius of painting folds of blue fabric and shadow, not to mention *light* and *thought* and all of that. She just *was*—a part of the wallpaper of the child's world that is indistinguishable from earth and sky. The baby in the painting was easier to see. He was bonny with a full-on gaze and lit just like his mother. But, back then, it was the woman who harnessed my attention. Her light seemed to emerge from thick night. I had no way of looking directly into her eyes. She was, somehow, less important. But without her, the baby would not be there at all.

Around the house where I lay in such glorious idleness, there was no landscape to speak of. Just acres of grey sky. The trees resembled dissected lungs for most of the year. The crows made their large black nests in them. I saw the path before me in the deep tread left by my father's boots. In the slime of wet leaves and the milky clouds of breath. As we walked, churches swung into view like ships in a flat brown sea. Their graveyards were stuffed with lichened graves; often, the village around them had been wiped out by plague. There was nothing of Mary in those churches, though many were named for her. The shrines and niches were empty. On one whitewashed wall hung a large black iron wheel, utterly detached of meaning. Hundreds of years before, it would have been spun by the sexton to determine on which of the Virgin's feasts a fast should begin or end. But there was nothing and no one to explain this. The ornate black circle looked, to me, incongruent and mysterious. As if it belonged to the ghostly carriage my grandfather swore he saw outside the church one winter's night.

How many glimpses of Mary I must have had without even realizing it. In my infancy and youth, she was my Old Testament: she foreshadowed the coming of Christ himself into my life. There was no God in my own home, no prayer. There was only an injunction to kneel to no one and nothing, and a right-sounding insistence that I would grow up to be successful and strong. But I saw that oil painting, an imitation of Raphael's *Madonna del Granduca*, on my grandmother's wall. I knew the name *Mary* as I knew the names of chaffinches, sugar-beet, and lily-of-the-valley. When I scrambled out of my grandmother's spare bed in the morning and looked out at the fields of charred stubble, I could have seen her, as the Scripture says, sitting at the gate. Hers was the hand that would lead me slowly to her son.

In that back bedroom, there was another, smaller picture of Mary. This time her skin had a sepia tone, almost mimetic among the rocks. Her expression was tender but remote to the point of coldness. I couldn't even have told you that there was a woman in the picture, or angels, or a baby. All the shapes seemed of a piece with the dull gold Florentine frame. The same way my life felt as one with the plowed fields and grey light.

But that was how Mary got in—not through statues or cute Christmas cards, not through prayers or teaching or through a historic wheel, but through those pictures. Mary got into my head against all likelihood, against the mighty determination of my father that our lives would be devoid of anything religious. She got in, just as a door that's slammed and locked and the chain pulled across cannot keep out air.

After my grandmother died, I asked Granddad not for the large Raphael of mysterious light but for the smaller picture of the sepia-skinned Madonna. It was her I wanted for my new room in the nurses' home in London. He gave me a fob watch too (my grandmother's had fallen to pieces) and instructions to find the house where they lived during the Blitz when she was a midwife and he a policeman. But I didn't put the picture on my wall: I kept it in tissue paper under my bed, in a suitcase crammed with letters and cassette tapes. It was a keepsake, a relic of childhood. Neither it, nor Mary, seemed to have anything to do with my life and the city I was trying to make home.

But my obsession with Mary's face only grew. Once I qualified as a nurse, I kept a picture of her in every room I lived in. My first published book of poetry contained several poems that mentioned her, and so did my second. Going through boxes of early manuscripts in my mother's attic recently, I was stunned to find crowds of references to her on yellowed pages.

Strange, then, that when I became Catholic at the age of thirty-nine, I didn't much feel Mary's presence. I was even a little dubious about the startling array of Marian devotions on hand and the never-ending reports of apparitions from all around the globe. Yet I continued to write about her. I was aware, after so many years, of the significance of Marian art in my life. But the messages she brought me through those images have taken decades to sink in.

Some see the past as another country or a station further down the railway line from where we've come. To me, it's a lit house at night. I've told the story of my life in many ways, but I have never managed to fully reveal the role of Mary within it. I have had to walk around the past, that "house in darkness," and peer through other windows to make sense of her quiet yet tremendous presence. Events I had thought finished reveal, hidden in a corner, away from the direct line of the front door, the most significant woman in history. As I walk the dark garden of memory, scenes of my life are witnessed from a new perspective. Some stories are tangential to my own. Some happened hundreds of years ago and involve people unknown to me; yet they are a part of my story, and hers, and in them I meet her face.

Any mother is more than a prosaic flesh-and-bones presence. She is a shape, a smell, a place, a sense of belonging. She is what roots us in the world. Mary's presence in my life has shape-shifted from image in art on my Grandmother's walls, to archetype, to historical woman, to something almost impossible to define. For the world, she is no easier to pin down: she is the New Eve; she is heralded by Sarah, Ruth, Hannah, Esther, and Judith; she is the bride in the Song of Songs; she is the New Jerusalem and the Ark of the Covenant; she is Wisdom personified. To some Protestants, she is a "glory-stealer." To feminists, she is a victim and a symbol of woman's defeat. To Catholics she is that seemingly impossible thing, the Mother of God. In my journey of discovery, I have realized that the tension between the woman of flesh and blood born in Judea more than two thousand years ago and her total essence is vital. Mary is simply a woman who lived and died. And yet she is, through this unique essence, far more. Misunderstanding this "more" leads to heresy (if we say that Mary is not the Mother of God, then we are denying the union of divine and human natures in Christ). It explains the Reformation rejection of her as an object of devotion (if we do not see Mary as Mother of God, then why would we revere her?) and the feminist fury about her (if we do not see that Mary's total obedience leads her to be the most powerful woman of all time, then we have to accept that she is a glorified doormat). But, as I hope to show through these stories, it is Mary's essence, and all that it entails, that holds the key to her indispensability in our lives. It explains how she haunts me, inhabits me, and pulls me on the only Way; how she so pervades our consciousness that she breaks through and into our culture no matter how much we deny and mistake her.

Our galleries are full of her. The Reformation couldn't begin to stamp out every image. Her face has been replicated thousands of times, by monks, masters, and even postmodernists. Yet the overwhelming feeling I'm left with—like Bernadette Soubirous when she looked at the statue at Lourdes—is that no one has got close to conveying what she is.

So how can I?

These pages can't contain a compendium of the Virgin Mary: *de Maria numquam satis*. They only attempt to delineate one sliver of her presence, her action in one life, in one person, and the impact on me of how others have engaged with her across the centuries, through art, distortion, piety, and prayer.

There have been, from the beginning, paintings and statues of Mary that have accompanied me. Some I sought out; others were given to me. The five artworks with which I subhead this "Prelude" and each chapter (*La Madonna del Granduca* by Raphael; *Madonna and Child with Two Angels* by Fra Filippo Lippi; *Our Lady of Guadalupe*, made without hands (an *acheiropoieton*); *La Pietà* by Michelangelo; and *The Statue of Our Lady of Walsingham* by an anonymous artist) have been the most iconic in my relationship with Mary. Their relevance to what was happening in my life is obviously idiosyncratic, but what they have taught me, directly and indirectly, about Mary has an uncanny and universal ring of truth. Interestingly, in all of the many works of art described in this book—even Chris Ofili's controversial Marian portrait made with elephant dung—inaccuracy and departure from who Mary really is have only helped me along in my journey to her.

I first wrote about Fra Lippi's *Madonna and Child with Two Angels* decades ago. But its message, through Mary, has continued to unspool. The tale begins in London, years after those weekends in the flatlands of Norfolk, in the room I returned to after a day working on the hospital wards. A room of one particular love affair, where the picture that my grandfather gave me was stowed in a suitcase under the bed.

Madonna and Child with Two Angels
by Fra Filippo Lippi, 1460–1465

ONE

New Eve

She is more beautiful than the sun,
and excels every constellation of the stars.
Compared with the light she is found to be superior,
for it is succeeded by the night

The London sky at night was never black. Polluted by streetlights and fumes, it was dyed in otherworldly hues of orange, violet, even green—which meant the birds, confused and exhausted, endlessly proclaimed the dawn.

The hospital where I was training to be a nurse was relentlessly wakeful too. As the dayshift went home, the sick, the mad, and the bad washed up to the gaping doors of the emergency room. Everything seemed to save itself for the night: babies were born, people died, patients fell over. Night was a place of intimacy and ungovernable pain, as though both patients and staff saved up what the day couldn't deal with. It was a time of skeleton staff and emergency prescriptions. Departments were closed, consultants were sleeping. An organ might be removed, or a violently psychotic man drugged to unconsciousness. We didn't have the luxury of team consensus or reflection. By the time the night staff handed over to the day, there was an abyss between them—the lack of empathy you find between two very different races.

"Have you seen that doctor?"

I heard of her before I saw her. In the packs of whitecoats standing at bedsides, she stood apart. She was slender, her skin was pale, her hair shiny black, her voice quiet, her lips full, her nose retroussé. Yet she wasn't what we might label as "beautiful" or "cute." She reminded me, fleetingly then, of my picture of the Virgin by Fra Lippi that I kept under my bed.

"I'm going to ask her out," said Mark, one of the male student nurses, over breakfast. We all hooted and someone spat their bacon out in hilarity.

"Different league, pal," guffawed John from Yorkshire.

But, male and female, we all liked watching her from afar. She looked kind, I thought, as she yawned at 3 a.m., writing drug charts, pager beeping, the charge nurse pulling at her elbow. Just kind.

The high-rise nurses' residence was home to hundreds of twenty-somethings, and we were all, in one way or another, looking for love. The corridors were full of sniffing, red-eyed girls who'd been dumped, or couples in their nightwear saying goodbye at the lift. Fevered mumblings and screams of passion pitched through the building at any hour; shrieks of despair and hurled plates were common too; and the bustle of nurses in heels and tight skirts screeching as they headed out to clubs. There were elaborate roast dinners cooked in tiny stoves at odd times and parties that blasted loudly for hours.

One day, a man, who I would only ever see in a police sketch, walked in the ever-open front door, took the lift to the thirteenth floor, climbed the stairs to the roof, and jumped. The last two or three seconds of his life were magnified by the paralyzed witnesses who saw him tumble past their windows: the physio and nurse making love, the student writing an essay at her desk, the Irish girl gazing at the cluttered London skyline and yearning for the green hills of Kerry. When I got home, the road outside was covered in yellow sand. To soak up all the blood, the policeman told me.

After a week, they brought a pencil sketch of the man to my door. I looked at it for as long as I could without seeming suspicious. I wondered if it was drawn from his corpse, grainy CCTV, or witness accounts. Was the calm, steady look in his eyes, the neatly combed hair, artistic license? Was it possible that a competent artist, by measuring what remained of a dead man's bones, listening to a passerby, or squinting at footage, could conjure true likeness and spirit? I thought of an artist I once knew measuring the nose of a woman with a paintbrush from afar, calculating the distance from the center of the eye to the bridge of the nose. It surprised me, then, that he was so concerned with mathematics. But it is only through careful calculation, he said, that we can light a fire. The wood has to be laid with great accuracy. It's the base structure that determines the color and shape of the flames.

We student nurses never found out who the pencil-sketched man was. But we recognized the city in him. We were all lonely; the wards were full of loneliness. The eyes of a Greek grandmother, who couldn't speak a word of English though she'd lived in London for thirty years, swarmed with misery as I washed her. Babies with thick legs or outsized heads had mysterious fits in dark rooms. There were overdoses and slit wrists; broken pelvises and elderly with no home to go back to. The psychiatric ward, where I ended up working, was home for months to a man with a briefcase and short pajama bottoms who was convinced he was president of the United States; a tall, handsome black man who thought he was Jesus Christ; Lilian, who performed ballet in the day room, her eyes opaque with madness; and Jen, who threatened to push me out of a high window. "I want to die, I want to die, I want to die," I heard over and over again. When I left the hospital after a night shift, I'd gulp life in the cold air, exhaust and roar of buses, the green smell of cut grass from the park, stale beer spilled on the pavement, baking bread and croissants. In the onrush of traffic, an old homeless man would be proclaiming the end of the world on a scruffy cardboard sign. A skinhead busker might play the saxophone, his notes tangling with car horns and the screech of trains. A conga of bald, orange-clad Hare Krishnas might weave through the rush hour, clashing cymbals and chanting. Occasionally, the image of a stranger—the beautiful doctor who we all watched, the Greek grandmother, the falling man—would magnify their lives to me in a disproportionate way, and I would feel the urge to reach out my hand and say, "I'm here!" or "No!"

She hastens to make herself known to those who desire her

On days off in winter, when there were fewer tourists and the parks were too cold to sit in for long, I took to walking around the National Gallery. First, I'd go into Saint-Martin-in-the-Fields for a lunchtime recital of Mozart or Shostakovich, then I'd wander over to the highly polished gallery rooms of medieval and Renaissance art, where I was met with silence, and room after room of the Virgin.

Those days, I'd pass, almost quickly, the clean somber lines of fourteenth-century paintings—the flat cracked faces by Barnaba da Modena, the wooden expressions of Giotto, the empty-window eyes of Cimabue. They seemed to leave me alone, with nothing. But I slowed at the blood and feeling in the faces of the Wilton Diptych. I bit on Lippo di Dalmasio's *Madonna of Humility* like a ripe fruit on a dry day; I pondered her fleshy love, her flushed complexion. Room after room I wandered, with no emotion, no words. The guard at the doorway sighed and checked his watch; tourists walked through as if surveying fields, something so vast you take it in on the move. I would always end in room 58, at Filippo Lippi's *Annunciation*, though I would not have articulated that this was my favorite, or even that I liked it. I was drawn to it, for reasons that seemed irrelevant and paltry— like the finely-drawn grey flowers, the colorful feathers, and the slow arch of the frame that enclosed Mary and the angel's bent heads. It was a shame, I reflected, that the subject was religious. But I had to admit, as I sat down and gazed, that in the lights and pounding of the city, here was silence.

It was about this time that I met Mischa.

I was working on a general ward, and all the patients in my bay were long-stayers who needed basic care and couldn't get out of bed unaided. There was the Greek grandmother who we called Yaya; a white-haired Irish woman who had a thousand shiny possessions and no means of reaching them herself; an Austrian lady who wore a diamond necklace with her hospital-issue nightie; and Edmund, who liked to stand to attention at his walker in the morning to salute me as I passed.

It was the hardest, quickest work I'd ever known. There were so many jobs and so much to organize that I took to trotting around with four thermometers and popping them in four mouths at once, then getting on with fetching clean bedding or taking blood pressure while they measured. Many was the time I'd go off on my break, to come back and find the four of them groaning and gurning, pointing frantically to the thermometers in their mouths. It was exhausting, the changing and making of beds and turning of patients. The knack of moving an un-sprung octogenarian from bed to chair on my own eluded me, and more than once, we both ended up on the floor. But the late mornings after ward-round, or in the late evenings as darkness lit the wards and drew us in, I loved perching on a bed to listen to tales of London during the Blitz or the bragging about grandchildren's prodigious talents.

"I was beautiful like you," the old women with bulbous noses and saggy earlobes often said. "I used to be as slim as you. You wouldn't believe it, would you!"

I didn't believe it. Their faces were smudged sketches of what they had been. Portraits eaten up by mold and damp. I gazed at them, trying to see their real faces, as I did with the sketch of the man who jumped. As I was beginning to do during my walks past all those pictures of Mary. What I was mining for in those paintings, in the patients I washed and changed, was the light in the eye or the particular tension in the mouth; something elusive but defining: the unchanging yet fragile place of identity.

When one day Mischa breezed onto the ward, I couldn't believe how ugly he was. He had crooked teeth and a weak chin. His eyes were murky grey, and his long hair, the color of dirty brass candlesticks, was shoved into a rubber band. But he made me laugh. He made everyone laugh. However dire the situation, when Mischa spoke, the eyes of consultants, nurses, relatives, and patients would glint; they'd rock with mirth.

When he saw me see him, that glint was multiplied and scatter-gunned through me. I was skinny, twenty-three, and brimming with expectation, like open water ready for lightning.

His face transfixed me. It was a strange face. I supposed that the reason I couldn't stop thinking about it was because it was so very unattractive. And then, as I examined it in my dreams, on the bus on the way into work, I began to conclude that it was beautiful.

"Write him a note and ask him out," my uncle, who was always deeply amused by my obsessions, told me over the phone.

"I wouldn't know where to send it."

"Well, it's a hospital, isn't it? Leave it with the commissionaire." My uncle was a playwright; to him, the world was one huge theater.

I waited until I left that ward, then sent a Greg Larson card to Mischa in the internal mail.

He called me one evening as I sat at my desk ignoring biology books and watching the Jamaican students in their hats and suits coming home from church. He thanked me, sincerely and gently, for my invitation for a drink—he was flattered, and *honored*, he said emphatically and with great care—but he had a "partner" (*a partner?* I thought, and wondered if he were gay). He asked me which ward I was working on now and how it was going, and then we hung up. I sat for several minutes with my face in my hands, his kindness burning through me.

One evening soon after, my Irish flatmates, Rosario and Siobhan, cooked a big roast in the tiny oven, and we drank several bottles of red wine. I couldn't bring myself to tell them about Mischa, but after hearing his voice address me so long and so carefully, I was still feeling paradoxically elated—triumphant and lucky.

"Here's to being lucky in love!" Siobhan toasted, her voice breaking open on the grain of cigarette-induced bronchitis.

Bach cantatas whirled out from my room and lit the flat, and smoke made it impossible to see our lamb and charred vegetables in the windowless hallway; we drank till we couldn't walk straight to the kitchen for a tall glass of London water. Siobhan, in her red satin nightie, her uncontained cleavage on her knees as she bent forward to lecture us, called for brandy, and Rosario trotted obediently off to get the bottle her brother had brought over the day before.

Siobhan tossed back a glass, and Rosario poured a good deal over a bought cake and lit a match. A blue flame roared up past our eyebrows then morbidly stroked the blackened sponge. Siobhan blew smoke rings and told us about her new man, a physio from pediatrics. They weren't having sex; it was all in the *sexual tension*. I knew what the term meant, but she labored it so much and wrapped it in so much theory that I was confused. "He's not yer man. He doesn't see you that way," Rosario kept saying. "It's *sexual tension*," Siobhan would argue. "The more he looks at me, the more we want each other, the more we don't do it . . ."

"And how long can this situation go on for?" Rosario interrogated, drably dressed and earnest. She and Siobhan were flatmates only because their aunts in Bantry were friends.

"He likes to *look*," Siobhan jabbed her cigarette at us. "He says I've got Bette Davis eyes." Her own laugh dragged her off her chair and onto the floor.

I didn't take any brandy. But when I fell into bed past midnight, the room was pitching, and I fell into a sleep that was more like a coma.

Deep in the night, the phone on the wooden desk beside my bed rang. I had the sense it had been ringing for a long time.

"Hello?"

"I woke you."

I knew it was Mischa. I have a terrible memory for faces (perhaps that's why they obsess me), but I can identify someone by their voice in a syllable. His was relaxed and dark. He never had to strain to make himself heard. The world was pulled to his words.

"No. Not at all." I blinked strenuously into the dark.

"What are you doing?"

"Reading the paper."

He laughed. "It's been an odd week. If you're really up, do you want to meet for that coffee? I don't want to bother you."

I switched my lamp on and looked at my watch, but the time was irrelevant.

I was up, downing as much water as I could stomach. I was pulling my jeans on, and combing my hair, and running up the hill to the hospital in the cold dark. It was no trouble. It was 2:30 a.m., and in the false orange dawn of the London sky, the blackbirds were beginning to sing.

❦

I knew who Mischa's "partner" was before I knew—a kind of déjà vu that belongs to the gut. "You mustn't think like that," he told me over the phone one evening, the way most of our conversations happened. "It's like when I was driving to my mother's for Friday dinner last week and this boy on a motorbike overtook me, bombing along. I thought: he's going to come off, and as I thought it, he did—skidded right across the road and was hit by a truck. Killed outright. He was only eighteen. But we don't cause things by thinking."

We don't cause things by thinking, but sometimes we just know. Knowledge lies like a wordless footprint across our mind, and then we see the foot swing forward to make the print that's already there. As if those paintings of Mary in the gallery were simple shapes awaiting her specific lines. Or mourning her departure.

"You're going to hell," Rosario might have said, had she known that the phone calls that came many times a day and through the night were from him. "Ah, go for it. Ya could be dead in the mornin'," Siobhan would have assured me, funneling her smoke out the side of her mouth.

"They're not married. They don't even live together," I reasoned to myself in the mirror. "This is the end of their relationship and the beginning of ours."

"No one's ever free," my uncle shrugged when I met him in a bar with deep velvet armchairs in Leicester Square. My shaggy-haired uncle was my guru on matters of love and literature. His cigarette was always lit; he was always listening. "People are always just out of a relationship, or in one, or chasing someone else," he told me. "There's overlapping, underlapping. No one is ever one hundred percent available. Doesn't exist. You have to stick your hand out into the traffic and hope."

The hot wind of London was stronger than my bones. It lifted dirt and flung it in my eyes. It funneled down into the tube where it lifted my skirt. It tangled my hair and raked my skin. Glassy-eyed with thoughts of Mischa, I stayed on trains beyond my stop. I forgot my pasta boiling on the stove, and Rosario came home to find the pan smoking. My mind was tuned incessantly to the phone's ring. If it didn't ring, I sickened; I physically stooped. But it did ring, and there was not one cell inside me that didn't ignite at his voice.

The first time, he came by late at night. "The only time it would ever be," he said, and slid my white cotton shirt off my shoulders. He told me this could never ever happen, and never again, never and never, over and over. "Never," repeated like a thing you cannot bear to put down.

He didn't kiss me at first. Neither of us believed (or had even heard of in a serious context) the notion that the body was a temple. But I knew that some prostitutes guarded their mouths, reserved them as seat of deeper intimacy and respect. And in giving me his mouth, or taking mine, I knew he felt he would betray his partner in a worse way.

I knew that she was the beautiful doctor who everyone watched. The one who had reminded me of Mary in the Lippi painting under my bed.

"Never speak to me of him," Rosario told me when she eventually found out. Rosario was somehow set apart from our shenanigans through those years. She was the cleaner-upper, the confidante, always in the kitchen with her arms folded and her head on one side. "I want no part of it," she said now. "I can't see her at work and know what's going on."

She couldn't understand this wind, I thought, this blindness, this compulsion. As weeks became months, the compulsion became worse, and so did the sickness. We were like Paolo and Francesca in Dante's *Inferno*, condemned to be dragged eternally by torrents of air. We were buffeted on sheer white force—up to Primrose Hill at night, among the weird bird calls of the zoo; on my tiny balcony among the giant chimney pots; down hospital corridors to some anonymous meeting room; in my bed. We would part, but he would be back at 3 a.m., the damp London night on his skin, his hair smelling of cold exhaust. We would break up, cry ourselves sick, meet for a sandwich to console each other two streets from the hospital. There's a painting by Gaetano Previati of Paolo and Francesca where they seem transformed into clouds themselves, borne up and scudding. Their motion never ends. Mischa and I were in ecstatic flux—calling, falling into bed, kissing, parting, waking, crying, laughing, calling, parting—and I thinned out, weakened but could not let go. "You're my *shiksa*," he would joke, "What would my mother say?" "*Shiksa* . . ." he would whisper, "hair like wheat, eyes of sky-blue, oy vey . . ." The tidal pull to each other seemed stronger than any existing tie he may have. Many times I assumed he and his partner had split, or were about to. Or that was the lie that I told myself. Patience was called for, I reasoned to the mirror. And he fed this patience. Wherever I was, he called me: at home, on the ward, at my parents' house. At a bed-and-breakfast in Stratford-on-Avon where I stayed alone one night, suddenly, at 11 p.m., there was a boy of eight at my bedroom door, holding out the family phone: "I thought if the play was good you'd want to talk about it," Mischa said without announcing himself. "And if it was bad, you'd want to talk about it too."

I listened to Mahler and Bach continuously; read Keats, Yeats, Eliot, and Plath; and wrote clumsy poems about the city and heartbreak. He bought me contemporary anthologies of women's poetry and collections by the body-bewitched New York poet Sharon Olds: "I'm going to drag you screaming into the nineties." He read my poems when he came up to my room, his doctor's bag at his feet and his eyes red from the nightshift.

"You're going to be a poet," he told me with his usual authority. And when I longed to be published, "Darling you will be. Even if it's on the side of a carton of milk, you will be."

Mischa and the woman doctor moved in together, then bought a house. They were bound, he said, not only by their history together, but by a deeper, more mysterious narrative. Both Jewish, they were *thinking with the blood*. I qualified as a nurse and moved into my own flat. But even when I no longer saw him, I still listened to the unreasonable song of my own blood; I was still tethered to the phone line. It seemed to have become an umbilicus, the only thing that gave me life. This story is old though. In that sense, it's uninteresting. The true story, the only reason that I tell it, is that it was the next chance that Mary took to step into my life.

In the wind and light of the city, I rested in a gallery of paintings of the Virgin. In the winds of that affair and its aftermath, I rested in one particular painting of her face. Mary's eyes in that Lippi painting, which I took out of the suitcase under my bed and hung for the first time in my new flat, were so like those of Mischa's woman: naked and sensitive. The woman shared with that fifteenth-century Madonna an entrancing look of poise, of pre-collapse. Her face lay across my mind with all the weight and type of a work of art—all the many things it said in its silence. When I saw her in the canteen drinking coffee alone, when I crossed her in the street and even said hello, I thought of that painting of Mary. Once, I sat beside her in a meeting and had an hour to memorize her court shoes and lilac silk scarf; the smudge of black eyeliner beneath her expansive brown eyes; the mascara clump in one epicanthic fold; how she braided her hair. And I saw Fra Lippi's Virgin's smooth forehead, the perfectly painted curve of her nose.

Mischa's woman seemed absolutely untouchable. As she endured, I seemed to crack. As she lightened, I seemed to darken.

As she did not seem to hear my phone calls, my brief entrance into their lives, my almost-plot-twist of her story, I became deafened by the roar of what bound me to Mischa, what would bind me for many years to come. I walked home from work every day, the yellow lights too loud, the buses vicious through the puddles. The cafés were full of lovers, and I felt a banging in my head, as if my thoughts could not be contained. There seemed to be a cool island of existential calm that, on the face of it, was inhabited by successful couples owning garden flats in North London. But beyond that, there existed a serenity that I thought I would never possess. Never.

Mischa still called. It was him I paged when I had my first poem published. It was him I paged when my father became ill. As Mischa and the woman set up home and my time with him began to belong to that shrinking place, the past, it seemed impossible that my indelible thoughts of us could stain the London sky with such violent colors; that they could consume my life.

"You look *desolate*," Rosario pronounced when we met for coffee, as though it were a medical term. *Desolata*, Dante would have said—abandoned—the word built around the Latin *solus*, alone. Even then, even in that moment, I saw the woman walk down the high street, past the window. I couldn't have felt closer to her if she had marched into the coffee shop, sat down beside me, and taken my face in her hands.

Then, one afternoon as I walked home from my shift, Mischa pulled up in his car beside me.

"Want a lift?"

It seemed so normal, getting into a car with him in broad daylight and driving down the high street among shoppers and the school run.

"You don't look well." He snatched quick glances at me as he drove.

We climbed up the carpeted flights of the large white house and into my attic room where I lay down on the bed, for no other reason than that the settee was miniscule, and I only had the energy to be horizontal. For months it was that way. The tears slid out of my eyes, but they meant nothing: there was no seam between crying and not crying.

He sat on the edge of the bed.

"I'm sorry. I'm truly sorry." He leant over me and kissed me, with love and apology, on the mouth. He carried on kissing me, almost without moving, as though someone forgot to move the secondhand of the eternal clock onward. We became locked together more deeply than I had ever known, and the tears carried on sliding down my temples. The fit of his mouth on mine was tight and perfect. I couldn't breathe. I felt myself become faint. And then I breathed, as if I had become amphibious and could stay underwater forever. I could open my eyes and see his eyes up close and unguarded, their hardening to black like a country night sky, which is really space, a dark window to something else. I could merge into his face; our thoughts melted and blended. The face: place of leakage, breathing, utterance, laughter, where every tiny thought or feeling ruffles, crinkles, darkens, lightens, like wind over a wheatfield; the place we are read and understood. I had never been entered so thoroughly as during that kiss; never been less alone. It seemed to be the most perfect way of knowing me. It was not only filled with pity; it seemed to *be* love; it was feeding and being fed. At the same time, it took the rest of me from myself.

When he finally sat up, the room was dark and the traffic slower; my neighbor had begun a piano lesson. I could taste blood.

I didn't get up to see him to the door.

It was some months after that encounter that, in search of solitude, I moved again. In my new flat in Mornington Place, I hung the Lippi picture on another wall. Like Mischa's woman, this Mary was as still as a pool of water. I could not begin to understand her. I couldn't understand the stillness of detachment, the stillness of prophecy. These were things I sensed the shape of but didn't yet have the vocabulary or wisdom to define.

So I began writing poems about Mary, or about this image that claimed to be her. Fra Lippi's Madonna suggested, more than anything, metaphor, not reality. In fact, the lady of this painting shared neither hair nor eye color with Mischa's woman, nor any woman in this world that I can think of. Her complexion was eggshell in both color and texture. Her drastically high hairline and sculpted eyebrows made her seem almost transparent. But her expression was now so familiar to me that it seemed to want to tell me something entirely human. Despite her ethereality, there was an inescapable sensuality in her jawline, her slight overbite, the succulence of arms and breast.

ii

Such a smile within her eyes
I thought the very depths of my own paradise,
my soul's innate glories, were present before me . . .

I have to go backward to circa 1456; to make an analepsis in Mary's journey to me; to leave, momentarily, the roar of London and my new stillness within it as I gazed at Lippi's Virgin on the wall. I was trying to look behind the paint, searching for Mary. But she is not so easily seen. We must stumble, first, on the woman modeling her, taking on—willingly, or unwillingly—that incomparable role. We have to imagine the windless heat of early September in medieval Tuscany, its lethargy and fruit, and hear a woman's voice across a courtyard from behind a shutter:

"You have the wrong woman."

Lucrezia is repeating these words over and over as Filippo Lippi wipes sweat from his eyes and frowns at the strokes of his brush on the canvas. ("Each hair is perfection!" he mutters to himself, not listening.)

Lippi painted her even when she cried silently or protested like this. He painted the smooth, high forehead, the curved nose, even that oh-so-human overbite—and in every particular, he seemed, or thought he seemed, to come, paradoxically, closer to the Mother of God.

"You think of nothing but flesh and paint," she would snap at him years later, and he would wonder as he rinsed his crusty brushes, "Don't I?"

28

The summer of those tears he was fifty—a friar-priest, artist, and bad-debtor—and had been commissioned by the nuns of Santa Margherita in Prato to paint a picture for their high altar. As he arrived one day in the sisters' chapel to take his measurements, the artist appreciated lazily the sight of the Dominican nuns in their long black habits filing in for midday prayer. Women were what Lippi loved. All women. And faces. He watched the holy sisters from the transept as they genuflected: the old and wizened, the spotty, the earnest, the chubby, the gaunt, the impossibly young. All were expressionless. They knelt and prayed with one voice.

"Only artists and religious would be expected to carry on working in this heat," he muttered in the near silence. Those last days of summer were dead: the market shut early. Even in the darkness of the chapel, mosquitoes needled his ears and the sweat ran as he watched the black-framed faces process in and out.

As he set up his easel, he supposed he could repeat himself in this painting. After all, he had painted Mary many times, and faces were what he was good at (*Not hands*, he shuddered). Even as a boy, he had sketched faces in the margins of his schoolbooks. (It was this that kept him focused as the priest droned on.) As he matured, "his Marys" had Masaccio's gorgeous folds of silk and shades of flesh—and something more: a magical light in the eye, an electrical charge in the muscle.

But perhaps it was the sight of all of those nuns' faces passing in front of him that made him ask himself again: *What on earth should the Virgin look like?*

The long line of women in black filed in and out of the chapel day after day as he sketched and mixed colors. It was only the third day that he saw Lucrezia. Perhaps she had been indisposed till that point; perhaps her downcast face had been hidden by her veil. That morning, the girl's luminously frank gaze seemed to still the already still street outside the open door. It lightened and darkened the sky, and silenced the sounds of feet on the grey stone floor. Beauty silences. It speaks of rightness. Looking at this fair girl, the last in the line of novices, Lippi froze, paintbrush clenched between his teeth like a bone. He could think of no better woman to represent the Virgin Mary in his painting. As he carried on working, the idea did not leave him; it grew. Then it obsessed him. It took days before he could persuade the Mother Superior for permission to use her as his model. In the end, dazed by the artist's hand-wringing insistence, she handed Lucrezia to him.

After terce each day, Lucrezia would hang back in the chapel with a much older nun. For two minutes, the pair would sit expressionless and silent, and then, without a word exchanged, kneel and begin reciting *Aves*. Lippi, who had set up his easel before the altar to paint in the same light where the picture would hang, walked in front of them, holding a paintbrush horizontally to his eyes to measure the young forehead and nose bridge. He dropped the brush vertically to take in her neck and bust. He moved to the side to assess the curve of her nose. As he watched he sensed, in the delicacy of her eyes, that she was acutely conscious of being watched. Sometimes he just stood, hands at his sides, and waited for her color to swell up from the inside, her blood to draw to his gaze.

Lucrezia had never been looked at so much by a man, barring Christ himself as he looked down at her from the cross. When the artist said, as he painted, that she was to be the model for the figure of the Madonna herself, Lucrezia had been profoundly confused: How could *her* face ever represent the Mother of God? There was no opportunity to ask this friar-artist that question, and she wouldn't have known how to phrase it if there had been. But she might have told him that she loved the vermillion of his Virgin's gown, which seemed like everything her body didn't know how to express. She loved the pale slivers of gold lying on a dish before the altar, cut so fine they were translucent, like bloodless tiers of flesh. She loved saying the *Aves* as Mary's outline appeared, and she longed for the face to come.

Lippi saw Lucrezia's face day and night, which he might have expected. He traced it in his dreams. He gibbered about it under his breath as he poured olive oil on his salted bread. It was not unusual, was even to be praised, this zeal to reach the truth of the Virgin. But, soon, the silence when Lucrezia entered the chapel hissed in his ears like the strongest wind. His hands shook as he painted. He watched her with a parched mouth. And then, just once, she returned his look for a second—without the black-habited nun at her side noticing anything—with just a dart of her naked eyes.

It was September 8, 1456, the procession of the Girdle of St. Thomas (which conveyed the belt, legend has it, that Mary let down to doubting Thomas as she was assumed into heaven) through the streets and piazzas of Prato. The hammering heat of afternoon had eased in the early evening, and the sisters leaned into the lengthening shadows as they walked. Lucrezia was at the back of the procession with another novice, praying out of sync with the group because they were so far from the front. Old ladies in black leaned out of their windows to throw petals and coins. Men on horseback cleared the way noisily at the front and reared up at the back. Children ran alongside the nuns, scooping up coins from the street. Men and women lined the narrow roads, eating slices of roast pork and fennel.

He never made any conscious decision. That is, the notion came to him, well mapped out, one night, and he brooded on it in the day and let it run in his head. But if he had been asked if it was what he planned to do, he most certainly would have denied it. At 8 p.m., he waited in a narrow street where the shadows converged and the procession thinned to two at a time. He made himself invisible in a doorway, and as the tumult of voices passed and she approached, he stepped out and blocked her way.

"Go!" he said to the open mouth of the plump novice beside her. As he saw Lucrezia step toward him and the beginning of a questioning smile, he bundled her back into the bright piazza and, with no little force, onto his waiting horse and back to his lodgings.

That night he drew her.

Despite the pummeling of tears and questions from Lucrezia when she realized the grave drama in which she found herself, despite the knocks of the Dominican sisters who had arrived at both his doors and every closed shutter at street level, despite yells and supplications and loud prayers, he drew.

"God is watching you!" one of the sisters in the piazza kept shrieking, over and over. "Give us back our child!" wailed the others, over again. As soon as the banging subsided, it would start up again louder than ever. Hundreds of *Aves* were prayed, loud, then quiet, fast, then slow, like the waves of an erratic sea. Lucrezia thought it would never end. But she somehow knew that, fierce as that sea was, it would not penetrate this house.

Lippi stuck his head out of an upstairs window, "Calm yourselves! I'll bring her back in the morning. I'm working on the portrait!"

"We'll call the *podestà*!" the mother superior threatened.

"Call whoever you like. I'm fulfilling my binding contract of work to you!"

He gave the girl a cup of water and yellow apricots on a plate that he'd picked from the courtyard that morning. Then he showed her where she could lie down in a cool room away from the hubbub. But she wouldn't move nor speak now. So he drew. What he had done scared even him. But if he drew her, God would understand.

"You should know," he told her as dawn leaked into the room and the shouts and knocking finally faded like the fever of a night's illness, "that I love you."

"You'll go to hell for this," she assured him.

"It's easier to have you here than come to the chapel every day. I have to spend time with you. I have to enter your face. Then I can work alone in the chapel."

"You're lying."

He was a terrible liar. His plump red face seemed to ooze his inner desires (for a woman, a slice of pork, or a nap), whether he needed to conceal them or not.

But I'm not lying, he thought to himself, *and not really sinning either. How can I resist this terrible force, this wind that carries me along without my feet even touching the ground? How can I know this face with pencil, paintbrush, and measuring? I can only know it with my hands, my lips.*

And so, like a blindfolded man, he approached her and touched her for the first time—her eyelids, her cheeks, her nose. She gasped, but kept perfectly still.

"Please don't worry," he was almost crying. "How can I understand you without touch? Look at you—as I watch you, you awaken. As I touch you, you come to life!"

"You have the wrong woman." She was crying too. "We'll both go to hell."

"Only this once. Never never never again. Never ever."

ꙮ

Lucrezia stayed with him. For some weeks, she remained immovable and mostly silent, and, if he were honest, those were the days Lippi enjoyed the most. He could see that she had no real desire to escape. He observed her minuscule reactions to his compliments, his words, the apricots he brought her. And when he touched her, she was soft as an apricot herself, malleable with consent. His guilt lay in the pleasure he took in her inner conflict and confusion. He had never known a face so transparent; every thought and emotion sailed across her pale cheeks and eyes. Pleasure, tiredness, distress, and desire all left the shadow of their bird-like footprints on her skin. It meant that, after some days, he didn't worry when she demanded to be taken back to the convent. The first time he took her, she did not even go inside—just arranged her shawl and veil, took a step, and turned back to him. But when they reached his house, she demanded he take her back to her sisters again. She told him that she feared for her eternal soul and was determined to return to her vocation. Yet it had only taken him to drop his reins and hang his head for her to say she would stay for the portrait—though only (rather conveniently, he felt) out of obedience to him.

"Tell me what to do," she took to saying every morning, gasping with tears. "I daren't see my parents. They say my father has never smiled since I left. I confess, then I walk right back here. God is turning away from me. I give myself to you, then I desert you. I give myself to God, then I desert him. I'm being destroyed."

Nothing he said could stop her tears. He couldn't tell her what to do. He couldn't confess her himself. He didn't have the strength to send her away. He could only draw her.

"Tell me what to do," she kept saying. Then she was quiet. He wondered if it was the Mother of God who truly entered her face then—she looked so much like her! All his life he had puzzled over whether the Virgin should be painted as blonde or brunette, knowing or naïve. Every human line of a face—every pert nose or determined jawline—seemed to block the essence of Mary. But anything more than human (he thought of the severe-looking icons he had seen on the Adriatic coast) negated anything we might ask from a mother. (He could not remember his own mother; it was her absence and the absence of his father that had landed him in a convent at the age of eight).

What calm would come upon Lucrezia as he sketched and watched and measured, trying to do what any artist tries to do: to express the inexpressible. Sometimes she would close her eyes and sleep sitting up, just where she was, like a child.

"No one knows me like you do," she smiled one day in early October. "You are my lover, my guide; you know the proportions of my body, the distance between my nose and lips, my eyes, the structure of my ear. You understand me like no one else."

Like God, she almost said, but stopped herself. Eyes popping, mid-mouthful, he looked scared enough.

By six months, she had taken off her veil and was shopping in the market and baking bread like any other woman of the town. By a year, she had become a mother.

ဢဢ

For years every afternoon, long after they left Prato, she submitted to being drawn and painted by him, and her face, in some sense, became Mary's: her consciousness of being watched became Mary's excruciating purity. Her excavated, adored, and inventoried beauty became Mary's, because all that is beautiful is hers, no matter how glancingly it touches on her. Lucrezia's look of being searched for, thirsted for, of being the quiet and open gate at the final destination; that is all Mary.

Like a spark on dry grass, one touch and the Virgin kindles, grows, inhabits, illuminates—even a brothel, even a sewer; certainly a love affair. This is what the Dominican sisters, who hung Lippi's completed paintings in their chapel, must have thought. This is what the people of Prato felt in their guts as they prayed—and so, anxiously, did Lippi.

Toward the end of his life, Filippo Lippi, the motherless boy, returned to Prato and sat before his painting of the Virgin in the chapel of Santa Margherita. He was in an agony of sorrow, hounded by debtors, accused of faithlessness by Lucrezia, broke. But in prayer, in the desolation of that morning and in the darkness of his own cupped hands, he thought he saw the Virgin's true face: the pure seduction of reproach and salvation.

She was nothing like Lucrezia.

Now he understood, as much as anyone can understand. The Virgin's look, her beauty, wasn't to be caught in bones, in flesh. It was more like the breath-stopping rosy light on a puddle in evening when shades are just about to change. As an artist, he knew those encounters with beauty so well. They escaped; he had to capture them. It was the artist's almost impossible task. The Virgin's beauty was a skein, a web, something settled on her and within her. It was more delicate than slivers of shaved gold, and more solid and vast than the earth's crust.

How could he possibly have found her before now, in this brokenness at the end of his life? Artists have all the right questions. They may even come closest to the right answers. But their closeness to truth can lead them into the greatest blasphemies.

How could I ever find you? he might have asked the Virgin as he knelt before the altar. *Painting you is like trying to paint an apricot from the Garden of Eden—a fruit that is the thought of God, unblemished, alive with his intention. Every other woman from Eve onward has lived in the gaze of men. Has been brought to life, in some way, by others. Has been bruised, lit, polished, nibbled, discarded.* He remembered Lucrezia's reddening cheeks in the chapel. The first sunny weeks of pleasure and cooking. *But you only live in the gaze of the Creator. You are so transparent, so artless in that gaze that you are like a mirror.*

The tremendousness of what that meant made him cover his own face with his hands.

৵৵

Five hundred years later, I saw in one of Filippo Lippi's pictures, not Lucrezia who modeled for that Madonna, not the Madonna herself, but Mischa's woman. I saw her delicacy, her high forehead, her fragile imperturbability.

We are drawn to liminal places—the line between wholeness and fragmentation. The building as it sways and shakes; the sky as it darkens and lightens and is broken by rain; the sense of being both destroyed and saved by a kiss; the virgin as she is taken from a street one September day; the fruit as it crosses from ripeness to rot. No one can remain so still and so silent as Mary in that picture by Lippi. No woman can stay as composed.

Mischa's woman must have shattered, one day or another, through half-guessed clues or a phone call overheard downstairs in the middle of the night. Lucrezia must have shattered, too, when Lippi, after giving her two children, refused to marry her. The smooth water of her Virgin's face must have contorted in pain at their twisted, soiled, too-human story. Did she heave and scream? Did she hurl a plate?

But did the artful transformation of Lucrezia manage to speak of Mary—a woman who stood in agony and wept but didn't fall?

As I wandered around the galleries alone in the days after Mischa left for good, I can't say I didn't find Mary. If we continue searching, even unconsciously, it means we are onto a scent. I would even say that Lucrezia, those blank icons, the Raphaels, Duccios, and Giottos are echoes of her. Poor, pale, miserable echoes. I struggled to spend a day alone without Mischa's gaze. The guards sighed and checked their watches. The tourists walked through. But Mary, like God, finds a way to be present in the most dismal of doorways.

iii

The ancient Paradise was but a figure of her

At the age of seventeen, I played Eve in a medieval Passion Play in the ancient abbey of our town. My costume was a long ivory gown with embroidered pinafore, and the script was all in Middle English. The play was organized by the town's historical society, and my Adam, who wore tights and tabard, came from a different and much posher school. We didn't get along well in Eden; the first man was visibly displeased with the scruffy-haired waif playing his helpmate, and he stalked the stage as though I was a walk-on hindrance. Our medieval words were stilted, and so were we. A few days before the performance, I invited my drama teacher in to watch a rehearsal. As she contemplated our Eden alone in the auditorium, I could see her frowning and making notes. Afterward, she clambered up onto the stage to speak to me.

"What you're lacking is a sense of wonder. Remember that, as Eve, all these things that you are seeing are *new*. *Everything* is for the first time. Everything is intense, defined. A tree is *the* tree, every flower is *the* flower. You've got to radiate *wonder*."

I didn't really understand what she meant or how I could convey it, but that afternoon I climbed a grassy hill at the back of the high school from where I could look out over the whole small town. It was a bright, clear day, and at the summit, I was far enough away from streets to be swamped in silence: the air was just a conveyor of sweetness and grass smells, buzzing insects and sparrow song. For a few minutes, I wandered around the meadow reciting my lines. Then I lay on my back and looked up at the tight pixels of blue sky, the clouds like wisps of hair unfurling in water. Then I rolled onto my front and examined every blade of grass, every daisy and dandelion, as though I had never seen them before. And almost as though I'd taken some kind of psychedelic drug, each blade of grass sprang into particularity. The veins revealed themselves in darker green. Each clover leaf offered up its map of circulation, a density of pores in textured emerald I could never have guessed. I could have fallen into the structure of one leaf and ignored the rest of the world. I was shocked at how much I usually missed. The air on my skin was like the silk scarves of someone walking past and around me; the hairs on my arms and scalp sat up in awe.

That hour on the hill, my perceptions were so altered, I couldn't account for them. I ran back down into the town, along the streets, and into the schoolyard to tell my teacher, grabbing the arms of juniors to ask if they'd seen her. At last, I spotted her, coming out of a classroom with her arms full of books, and rushed up to her. But I stumbled on what to say, how to explain what happened. She listened though, and I think, in the opening up of her face, in her smile, that she knew. She was one of those rare teachers who *know*.

As a student actress, I hoped that the light of that hill would remain in me as I walked the stage in my ivory gown with my disdainful Adam. Thirty years on, it seems unlikely that it did. But I do believe, now, that I carried that awareness of purity—and its opposite, a sense of contamination—with me in the years that followed. I was aware of the danger of taking things for granted—the way that everything that we see is imbued with what we expect to see. Even then, I knew that it is a rare gift to see naked truth. I knew that every carelessly drawn image robs wonder and newness from us. If you had asked me, even then, I would have known that such a multiplicity of images of Mary as exists in our world can only hide her true nature. Unless we continue looking hard and ask all the right questions.

After Mischa, I kept the Lippi picture hanging up by my door, and for many years, in various ways, Mary's presence continued to weigh on me—and, even more so, her silence.

I complained to bemused friends that in the paintings I saw of her, her mouth was always shut (I'd only seen Botticelli allow the parting of sensual lips.) Her eyes were always downcast or raised to heaven. In Camden's Our Lady of Hal (where I sometimes peered, out of almost voyeuristic curiosity, on my way home with heavy shopping), she was unwrinkled and anodyne as a plastic doll. When I traveled home to East Anglia at weekends, the churches, which I stopped in on during my walks across the flat fields with their charred-looking trees, were full of cold vacancy; her statues were burnt.

She was silent. But I was nearer to finding my own voice. There had been one last phone call with Mischa. I was traveling back late from a meeting in Liverpool when the train broke down. We were stuck for hours between stations and finally rolled into Paddington at 1:30 a.m. The tubes had stopped working for the night; there was a stampede for taxis and not a bus in sight. Mischa was the only person I knew in the city who had a car. I thought about my long vigil for him, my silence, my unfaltering obedience in never contacting him at home. I called him from a payphone.

"Hello?"

"It's me. Can you pick me up from Paddington station?"

"What? Wait . . ." I could hear him moving into another room and carefully squeezing a door shut.

"What's going on?"

I told him.

"Listen," he hissed, "you've got a boyfriend now. Call him. You're putting me in an incredibly difficult position."

I slammed the receiver down and marched back to the queue of waiting hundreds.

Next day on the ward, I called Mischa's cell phone and left him a message. I'd begun a degree course in literature and was reading the feminists. In fact, the whole critical method was centered around the deconstruction of hegemony. It may not have served my literary tastes well, but it gave me a voice now. I told him he had abused me, had kept me in a box, had effectively silenced me and taken my right to ask for anything in return. I had been the embodiment of everything feminists hated about Mary as they understood her: I had been submissive, voiceless, unconditionally adoring. Well, enough. My relationship with Mischa had been, I realized, a kind of slavery. The diminution of his phone calls and visits had, after the initial shock, given me new and reeling possibilities, and I'd realized something vital: my bondage to Mischa had been a way of avoiding life; more, it had been a way of dying. Well, now I was no longer tethered. I was going out when I liked. I could turn out the bedside light without wondering when or if he would call. I could go and stay with a friend without worrying that he wouldn't be able to reach me. I was existing outside of his gaze, and it was sweet. It was almost living. I told him to never, never call me again. Never ever.

My flat in Mornington Place was given to me for a knockdown rent by an art therapist, Moira, with whom I worked for a while. She lived in the other two stories of the house and chose to rent out the ground floor to a series of financially challenged writers. The Georgian mid-terrace was solid, hushed, and decked out with thick cornflower-blue carpets and blue willow china. It smelt of paraffin and lavender. There were no computers, answering machines, televisions, or central heating. My sitting room had a gas fire that roared and ticked, but the sash windows were so gappy that the wind lifted my hair as I knelt beside it. About twice a year, Moira would come to my door, huddled in a shawl, to invite me up for sherry by the fire. Sometimes I bumped into her in the hallway: "What has happened," she might whisper urgently, having not seen me for two months, "to the past tense? It's been annihilated by trendy historians on the radio. . . . 'The great fire of London is burning.' . . . 'The Turkish fleet approaches.' . . . It's an affront to language, to history . . ."

Apart from that, I only saw her through my kitchen window in the evenings as she tended her pink and white roses, hollyhocks and tulips in the walled garden. It was there, in my kitchen, with the roses like bright moths in the dark and trains to Euston screeching home nearby, that I settled to writing. After years of wrestling with poetry and having a few pieces published in small magazines, I was finally writing poems that lived. I felt like Philomela given back her tongue.

The French feminist Hélène Cixous seemed to speak for both me and Mary: "Woman must write her self: must write about women and bring women to writing, from which they have been driven away as violently as from their bodies—for the same reasons, by the same law, with the same fatal goal. Woman must put herself into the text—as into the world and into history—by her own movement."

When asked why all her books were so short, the Italian writer Natalia Ginzburg replied that she grew up in a house with loud brothers; if she wanted to say something, it had better be brilliant and quick. I recognized my own upbringing: the essential rapidity of my speech, the pressure to reach the punchline. I read Charlotte Perkins Gilman's *The Yellow Wallpaper* and, unlike its incarcerated heroine, felt that I had imprisoned myself. I'd had to break self-imposed constrictions to flee the attic room where I had lived so closely with the telephone. Now I had to make my voice so acute, so at one with, and yet so at odds with, the noise of the world that people would lay down their knife and fork, would put down their newspaper. Just for a second.

I wanted them to recognize themselves in what I'd written. I wanted to mine words so deep that the truth stung. To harness attention so violently that they could not look away. My models were many: Sylvia Plath, Adrienne Rich, Sharon Olds, Anne Sexton, Germaine Greer, Kate Chopin, Emily Brontë, Simone de Beauvoir, Jorie Graham, Jean Rhys, Francoise Sagan, Hélène Cixous, Djuna Barnes, Virginia Woolf, Doris Lessing, Edna O'Brien, Margaret Atwood. I felt I was waking up to centuries of the conscious and unconscious blinding, muting, and general disabling of women. My poems became vivid, graphic. *Write through the body*, Cixous exhorted me from down the decades. But it was more than simply being feminine in what I wrote (instinctive, uncontrolled, driven by deep associations); it was using the body—its pains and desires—as expression of my story. I felt as if my skin was the pages on which were written Mischa's control, my complicity and eventual escape.

Mary's story needed to be told too, I concluded. Her hovering presence in art galleries, on postcards, in England's rare shrines seemed to lie in wordless but unmistakable opposition to my tardy awakening, my battle to never be silenced. I thought that I had taken the Virgin's hand; that I was leading her as well as myself, and the whole of oppressed womankind, to freedom. I was determined to tell her story. What happened on that simmering day of an angelic visitation? What act of love or violence had been obfuscated or untold in the careful wording of Luke's Gospel? Mary's story had been edited, reworded, and pushed into oblivion. I imagined her as the woman in the Song of Songs. But in my vision, it was a human love that she was searching for in the streets at night. I recognized her passion, her restlessness, in myself: "Have you seen him whom my soul loves?" This, I thought, must be the Virgin's voice: a young woman caught out by her own desires, forced into a monumental lie and lumbered with a child.

Writing took on a religiosity. I woke at 5:30 a.m. and strode swiftly to the top of Primrose Hill from where I could take in the long low city, all green in early mists, and the aviary nets at the zoo like giant cobwebs strung between branches. Then I marched straight back across the Victorian railway bridge with its brambles of cast iron, pausing to look at the yellow light. Back in my little flat, I wrote until it was time to go to work. I wrote blindly, stringing words with no real method, hitting sometimes, in a way that was almost accidental, on truth. In the evenings, I often took a walk in deeper yellow light around the base of the hill, past the large pink, white, and blue houses, one with a wooden rocking horse in the window, one with a piano, to Fitzroy Road where Sylvia Plath ended her life. I paused more at the red postbox at the end of the short road than at the house. Which poems were mailed in that slot, I would wonder, which letters of explanation? I imagined the dark-haired young woman pushing a stroller through deep London snow, which now seemed Narnia-like, unthinkable. But it wasn't her suicide that drew me. It was the fact that there, or nearby, she had managed to strike the tuning fork of language right so many times. And in the face of that offensive rightness, no one could turn away.

Mary's countering silence weighed on me.

Among the preachers pontificating in Trafalgar Square, she was silent; among the proclamations of the Catholic Church and the increasing chatter about a female priesthood, she was silent; in discussion and debate about women's rights, abortion, contraception, forced marriage, genital mutilation, date rape, and domestic violence, she was silent. It was men who silenced her, who took her story and used it for their own dubious means. It was men who robbed her of her sexuality, her desires, the ordinariness of her body, her pregnancy—the very truth of her story. How best to shut a woman up? Put her on a pedestal and give her a crown.

Not just the Lippi that my grandfather gave me but a panoply of Marian images began to inhabit my flat. Glittery Mexican prints, Byzantine icons with lizard-like eyes, a postcard of a modern Madonna in a long blue dress standing on a window ledge in Ely Cathedral, holding her arms up as though about to dive. Art had, more generally, arrived in my life. My new boyfriend was a young photographer from Newcastle who photographed corners of the city at unexpected angles, found form in neglected spaces and beauty in the accidents of collapse and utility. Our first week together, he gave me Hemingway's *A Moveable Feast* and took me to markets and galleries in the East End of London I never would have found. Whatever the faults in our alliance, we had in common the scorched impetus and desire to create. He had been living in the city for only eighteen months but knew it far better than I did. He had the tourist's list-checking scrupulosity and the historian's attention to narrative and detail. He knew the North-South-East-West of the city and was aghast that I always traveled by tube and got lost wherever I was: "You're moving around in the dark." He knew the wavy line of the river by walking it, the new tall buildings, and the dirty rose gardens and medieval churches they drowned out. He knew which trains to avoid in rush hour and the exact street to duck down when footfall thickened to unbearable limits. He had a voice that was as deep as a broad and hard-to-carry wind instrument, and was thick in the torso. His affection for me was always in doubt, but he liked going around with a poet, however lost, and I liked the fact that he would shamble up to where we were meeting—in a café, bar, or park—collapse into a seat, throw back a coffee or beer, untie his shoelaces, and begin, "Here's the thing . . ." "The thing" was the plan, the tracks his life was running down, the project, the goal, the art. Like two trains, we were both running, and for those months we were parallel, sometimes even companionable, before we lurched off in different directions.

At weekends, we set out across the grubby grey city from Camden, through Trafalgar Square, down into Horse Guards, along the river. We took pictures of a weeping muse at a Victorian monument, a broken concrete stairwell near Bank Station, the shape of a blown-out window against the sky by the river's silty edge, an intricate tree of cracked white paint on a door. We'd walk for hours, finding ways of seeing—beached tires by the water, a broken gate that hung like a flag from its hinges, stacked pub signs covered in ivy, and a pile of chains rusted into one immovable mass. There might be a red line painted across a pavement and down a curb, for no apparent reason. A green beer bottle wedged into a moss-covered wall. The word "FOREVER" painted under a bridge, long drips of paint running down like stalactites and blackened by fumes. Urinals, dead sharks, unmade beds—by the 1990s, all these things were art. The creative burden was in the eye of the beholder.

One Saturday afternoon, we went to an art-book party in Charing Cross Road, where young artists and shop people stood around drinking white wine out of plastic cups and making as many connections as possible before fleeing into the dying afternoon. I was introduced to an artist and his girlfriend who'd just returned from Paris and were full of plans about painting portraits from photographs of women. The artist's speech was stumbling and his fingers trembled. An unlit rolled cigarette stuck to his bottom lip, and his lashless eyes were reddened and unfocused. He couldn't stop kissing the head of his curly-haired girlfriend, who hung off his shoulder, tenaciously gazing at his stubble. In a distant way, the artist wanted to know about my poetry and what I was doing there at the party. (He couldn't seem to make sense of my presence, though I kept pointing to my boyfriend, who was off in a corner, pontificating to someone in his deep voice about "the thing.") When I started talking about my interest in the way that women are seen, and about images of the Virgin Mary, he put his plastic cup of wine down and pulled away from his girlfriend. Would I do a couple of sessions as a head model? He had a student that he was teaching to paint in oils, and it would pay well. Maybe it was vanity that made me reach for my diary. Or some artistic sense of adventure. I was enthralled by the suffering beauty Elizabeth Siddal, who had shivered fully clothed in a cold bath as Millais painted his *Ophelia*. And Jane Morris with her otherworldly pomegranate in Rossetti's *Proserpine*. Those women seemed to climb from the frame with their presence. It was what I wanted from Mary—and, I guess, from myself. Anyway, the sum the artist named was indeed unusually good, and as it was only my head that he wanted, I agreed.

One wet black evening soon after, we met in a bar near Liverpool Street full of office workers guffawing at the end of a long day cooped up. Bass-heavy music; neon-streaked rain through the window. In a beany hat and dustman's overcoat, the artist slouched in the corner of a seat as if sheltering from a storm, and let me get the drinks. He didn't speak when I returned. He stared at me with ludicrous intensity—not in the eye, or not entirely, but all over my face, and didn't answer my faltering small talk. He drummed on the table and stared at me some more. Downed a shot. Then stared again. When he got up to order more vodka for himself, I shuffled to the edge of my seat, wondering if I should make a run for it. But then he returned, and I told myself there would be other opportunities to back out— between there and the door, between street and destination. My body got up when he did and followed him out of the green- and yellow-streaked bar, but my mind was crouched and ready to run. We walked in silence down the empty street and into a backstreet and a tall office building.

There was a doorman reading a newspaper at reception, and I almost gasped with relief at the sight of him. I gave him a big, meaningful grin, knowing full well that his presence, many floors below where I would end up, meant nothing, really, for my safety. Again, I almost turned back and ran as the lift doors opened. I don't know why I so weakly got in. The artist was still silent, and I knew that now everything rode on what the other person in this deserted building, the painting student, would be like. After a long, uncomfortable ride, the lift stopped, and we walked down a dark corridor and into a room that was completely vacant apart from a chair.

As I sat down, the artist stood by the window rolling a cigarette, and then another set of footsteps became louder in the corridor, and my face and hands became hot: I had nowhere else to run.

And then he was there, in the room with us: a nervous, nice, normal banker in a grey suit, taking off his tie and apologizing to me about everything from the weather to the late hour. He clearly found the artist as odd as I did. He wanted to learn how to paint. That was all.

He and I bonded over our jitters and joked around as the artist set up light and easels and showed me how to sit.

Relieved, almost euphoric, I sat still under the hot light for a long time, soaking in my view of the black city with its skin of winking yellow lights. I looked at the neon tubes and signs for coffee and hamburgers so long I could hear my neck creak and feel my eyelids become thick and heavy. Men and women, never children, were marching fast, heads down, up and down the street. Going for trains and buses, meetings and meals, their umbrellas like colorful membranes, shrinking and twirling. I could feel my thoughts and emotions drain from me, pour out of me and over to the artist and his student as they drew, speaking in quiet voices. My bones took on the weight of stillness that wheezes and moans on the inside, that says: the body can't ever be still.

Be still. When I walk into the National Gallery in London these days, there is an air of being in a church (more so there, even, than in some London churches). There is richness, hush. The intimation of a presence. In one alcove alone, the weather changes yet further. The sky darkens. A strange night colors everything, yet leaves it visible. In this painting, the Virgin's skin is grey. Flowers are etched in dusk. Angel and babies are drooping with the deepest contemplation. The Virgin's cloak-lining is a streak of color like the choicest honey. And her face, hewn like rock, sculpted like marble, speaks the miracle of shaped bone. Her eyes seem to contain the world. They hide more sky than the sky behind them. The eerie divinity of the piece is unmistakable. Tourists quit their skittish whispers. I see a Japanese man bow before it. I cross myself.

Da Vinci sketched the woman (which woman?) in that painting, *The Virgin of the Rocks*, just as I was being sketched then. He pulled his Madonna from some unknown person. And somehow—despite his flaws, despite the flaws of the woman—he hooked an essence (not *the* essence, but an essence) onto canvas.

To some Muslims, the creation of images of living beings is blasphemous, even evil. Only God can be such a creator, they say. Poet and playwright Karol Wojtyła also recognized the risky and electric closeness of divinity and humanity in the creation of art. He knew that this territory is hair-raising—that it reaches for transcendence but can only ever be performed by artists as *instruments* of God, the ultimate Creator. In other words, artists don't create; they harness and shape what God has given them. Nevertheless: "None can sense more deeply than you artists, ingenious creators of beauty that you are, something of the pathos with which God at the dawn of creation looked upon the work of his hands."

How much God (a God I did not, then, believe in) must trust us in giving us these artistic gifts; how much he risks.

After two hours, the artist and his student in the empty building said that they were done. They were ready to look on the work of their hands. I stretched and collected myself as they pored over what they had accomplished, then turned their canvases to me. The student's was still half-finished, mostly in pencil. But the artist's was, almost miraculously, complete. There I was: red lips, red scarf, violet thought across a pensive face. The light in the epicanthic fold that sparks life. How did Lucrezia Buti feel when her lover turned the canvas to her? I felt robbed and adored.

The artist wanted to know if he could paint me naked.

ممم

I spent many weekends with my photographer-boyfriend. Over lunch in Soho, he met my uncle, who, cigarette lit, listened closely to his childhood tales of bare fistfights in Gateshead. My uncle listened as though he were listening to the only person in the world (as he did with anyone who had a story to tell). My boyfriend talked as though he was the only one with a tongue. He even took the train home with me to meet my mother, and spent the evening with me on the swinging seat in her garden looking up at the East Anglian stars. He loved the stars, the beach, my dog. But things were souring between us.

Sitting outside a restaurant one summer night in Camden, we got onto the topic of censorship before we had even ordered food. He already saw me as old-fashioned and somewhat fey, with my new Raphael Madonna above my fireplace and my absent-minded tube rides in the dark. He made it his business to introduce me to Jean-Michel Basquiat, Joseph Beuys, and Henry Miller. It was also through him I got to know something of pornography. Like most men I knew, he viewed pornography regularly and saw it as an entirely benign recreation that sat well between his first whiskey after work and dinner. As the internet swelled and let loose in those early years, no one, it seemed, was immune from seeing other people having sex. But there were some images so graphic and violent that even the most porn-habituated men confided to their wives and coworkers that they couldn't ever be rid of them. A friend's husband kept waking at night slick with sweat, and once sat up in bed and retched. He wouldn't tell her what it was he saw online, but she identified the burnt shape of something ghastly stamped in his eyes. Some things, she told me, brand your consciousness, and the scar never fades.

"Are you seriously telling me that *as a writer* you're in favor of censorship?" the photographer sneered now, and looked around the café and street as though he were already cutting loose from me.

"With some things, yeah."

The main course hadn't yet arrived, but now he was tying his shoelaces.

"Some things? Some? Things? That *is* censorship. That's what it is! Like what? Like what would you ban?"

"I don't know." I saw, with dismay, that, to him, I was falling into the polar opposite camp—conservative religious—but I was neither of those things. "Violence? Bestiality? Murder?"

"Oh, hell. Well, for starters, murder is a crime already . . ."

My thoughts were as loathsome to him as Nazism. I tried to articulate what I believed about chaos, order, and gatekeepers. But as with so much in this man's ideology, complete opposition to censorship was a deal-breaker. He was dogmatic about what constituted cool and liberated and what did not.

Even from the little of what I had seen online, I knew that pornography was now no longer a question of a consenting woman and a consenting man being filmed having the kind of sex that could make a baby. Even the idea was laughable!

Pornography meant distortion of the norm; it was defined by extremity. Each online image begged another image, a more dangerous image. Each scene paled after several views. The brain needed more, an extra dopamine hit. Like a heroin addict, the more it got, the more it hungered for.

As I sat there with a man I theoretically would have hitched (for the art, the books, the walks), I couldn't verbalize why there should be imposed limits on porn. I could only point to the growing anemia of our own sex life. And, of course, I couldn't do that.

When I reached home alone that night, I knew the relationship was already over, and I felt exhausted. There were purple-checkered tulips in bloom in the lamplight on Moira's doorstep, each petal covered in small, perfectly geometrical squares of color. It seemed almost unearthly to find such beauty in the city, but in that small street, I could often hear my own footsteps and, at night, a blackbird's song. I passed into the dim hallway and was again folded into the quiet creakiness of the 1940s. Moira was there, returned from the theater in a mac and navy ballerina-length skirt, her thick hair almost covering her glasses.

"Oh, hello . . ." She sounded bewildered to see me. "Raskolnikov . . . yes . . . what did you make of his confession?" She gathered up a stack of letters and postcards (one of Mary—a Bellini, I think) from the hall table.

"Oh, it's years since I read *Crime and Punishment*."

"Really?" She sounded deeply shocked. "Would you like to come up for a sherry tomorrow evening? About six?" She turned and climbed the stairs slowly before I could answer.

Halfway up, as I was going into my rooms, she turned again. "Oh, I read some poems of yours. Very vivid. Gosh. Yes. . . . Bravo." She laughed absently and continued her climb. I could never put an age to Moira and had never been able to wrest any

love story out of her. She was Catholic, I gathered from her cop-
ies of *The Tablet* on the hall table, and somehow virginal. Yet
she was—in the face of my writing, my goings-on—strangely
unshockable.

"Oh!" she stopped at the next stair. "Men are coming tomorrow about your shower."

I cringed. The weight of the photographer had broken the
shower floor.

"Are they going to rip it out?"

Moira's eyes widened in serious alarm. "Remove it gently,
Sally, remove it gently." And she ascended.

ॐ

I was excited. I was coming closer to seeing Mary liberated. A
new exhibition had come to London, and its most controversial
artwork was a portrait of Mary that would ignite much fury in
the US. The Virgin sexualized, it said in the papers. Her breast
exposed. Her angels made of cut-out pornographic images. And
the Virgin herself partly made of elephant dung. I was unsure
of this but felt, somehow, that serious art sanctified whatever it
touched. And wasn't any extreme measure called for to get to
the truth of this woman? I decided to make a day of my visit.
It was raining. I felt free, single, singular, powerful. I stopped
for a coffee at a Greek café and loved that no one knew who I
was or where I was going. I gave the guy behind the counter a
smile and told him to keep the change. I wrote lines of a poem.
I walked, got drenched, and carelessly picked the head of a wild
rose through the railings of a square. The world was reclaiming Mary, taking off her virginal blue cloak and giving her back
her power. Modern art was meeting her, and it would free her.
Walking home from my uncle's after lunch, I would blindly navigate the hanging fabrics and stalls of vegetables down Edgeware

Road. The covered women in their ballooning black burqas would ignore me in my short skirt and boots, just as I ignored them—as giraffes and gazelles ignore each other.

I didn't know, as I walked into the gallery and searched for Chris Ofili's *The Holy Virgin Mary*, that the bald fact of any nudity on Mary's part should not shock a Christian. But the truth is that the Virgin wasn't always covered up. The fourteenth-century German artist Hans Baldung Grien (who liked drawing naked women, especially witches) was just one of many artists who painted the Virgin breastfeeding. Was he showing the reality of the Incarnation? Was he inciting the viewer to a more tender love of God? Was he remembering Jesus' request (so touching we forget it, so incendiary it burns our eyes and we don't see it) to be his *mother*? In Grien's painting, Mary is not actually in the act of feeding the already satiated baby (who is lumpish with warmth, like a sack filled with sand). He has fallen asleep, his mouth molded by the shape of her teat, his eyes haunted with slumber. Even the curly angel at her shoulder has nodded off on the job: he clutches a bunch of black grapes like a teddy bear, letting the weight of his head fall onto his chest. But Mary gazes sleepily, just short of the viewer, like a woman so in love, or so tired, that she isn't aware of her nakedness. Or perhaps this is the medieval version of the lightning-speed snap: a single moment— the child's mouth falling away from the mother, her hand still tilting the breast to help keep him latched on—caught in laborious days of painting. Whatever the case, one white, plump breast and shoulder are shockingly nude—so nude that any modern woman might balk at revealing the same. But I didn't know about this kind of Renaissance art. The Virgin's nudity, with so much else, was rejected by the iconoclasts, and from then on, she was almost always robed in muffling blue. As I walked into a late twentieth-century gallery, I thought that Marian nudity must be groundbreaking. A guard pointed me to the room, and when I saw Chris Ofili's Madonna, I felt—nothing. Every response was taken from me.

ᘒᘒ

I'll share a secret. It's not nice, and you'd probably rather not hear it. It's one of those awkward details that rightly get suppressed by memory and left out of books. And yet, it somehow belongs here.

Around the time I played Eve in the Passion Play, I developed an infection that was extremely uncomfortable and ruining my rest. I was a virgin and had never before seen a doctor about anything so embarrassing. It's almost impossible to view certain events reliably through the kaleidoscope of memory. I remember certain details that now seem odd and unacceptable, like the fact the doctor examined me without a chaperone. (Was the examination even necessary?) I also remember strange comments he made, which at the time made me feel unclean and blamed, but which I didn't understand. "What have you been doing?" was one. I couldn't understand the inference (and still don't—it was a common yeast infection). I can't say if the medic was out of line, but I felt jarred, degraded. It was the first time I was penetrated.

On the Passion Play's opening afternoon, I looked out into the audience from the stage's wing in my long ivory gown and saw that same doctor—large, tall, bearded—at the center of the audience. A shadow ran through me, cleaving the newness and wonder I had created in our Eden from degradation and confusion. This shadow separated humiliation and trembling from a cool retreat into myself and a reality I was determined to be faithful to. My choice was clear: I could either blush, letting the irony of having been seen naked as Eve by this man crush me; or I could stride out there and ignore him. I did the latter—my look, I think, as I swept the stage in wonder, a little like Mary's in that painting by Hans Baldung Grien: absorbed, unfazed, but more distant than the moon.

໐໐ຂ

One rainy morning, I returned to the posh building in the East End to be painted naked. The artist brought along his girl-friend, and she made me coffee, chatted, and seemed to want to ensure there was no fear or weirdness about the day. We, the artist and I, had met in a café the week before to discuss our reasons for doing what we were doing. He was intent on looking at women—even in ugliness, even in crudity or pornography—and reclaiming their objectified form for art, for beauty, in oils. I was intent on women reclaiming their power by showing simply what they were, without covering, without apology, without a disabling modesty or attempts to conform to what the viewer wanted or expected to see. I (like so many women) felt crushed by the uniqueness of my form. I was convinced that I was seen as ugly by wider society. I would be weeded out before the swim-suit catwalk of the beauty pageant, the one to disappoint as I was unwrapped. The agony of this knowledge was, for me, not to be tolerated. Rather than feeling I should cover up, I wanted to rip off what hid me. I was convinced that if every woman showed herself as she really was, all of this body-depression and shame would evaporate. We might even find the true Mary; we would free the occluded woman. The artist nodded as I talked, as though he understood perfectly.

The far wall of the top floor was covered in windows, and in daylight it seemed as though we were all standing on a shelf ex-posed to the street and buildings outside. It was an odd feeling, removing clothes in a large room when no one else was doing so. The artist and his girlfriend were both silent when I stood naked before them. It was as if they didn't expect what they saw, and, suddenly, even they didn't know what to say or do. As if even they were shocked by this sudden rupture of rules. As if my body broke every expectation in the ugliest way, just as I expected it to do. We, all three, stood awkwardly in silence.

What else could I possibly have expected as I stood naked before two strangers?

ᖫᖬ

To be seen in my totality: my past, my present, my future; my mistakes and fault lines visible as scar tissue and soft as dying petals ready to fall; my deep and incontrovertible beauty (that, surely, everyone possesses); my preciousness, bravery, and pain. Does that seem too much? (I'm laughing.) In other words, I was trying to be seen as only God can see us. The way that Mary is seen, because she lets herself be seen that way. The way that Filippo Lippi was trying, so clumsily, to see.

That's what I was trying for in my feminist statement of "Here I am." I was aching for the sweep of divine attention that Adam and Eve knew so well in Eden; I was craving absolution and acceptance. Without knowing it, I was crawling my way toward prayer. Without having the least idea, I was dreaming of blameless, glorified bodies—Christ's in the garden when Mary Magdalene couldn't recognize him. And didn't she, the Virgin Mary, in her earthly life, contain something of that unimaginable glory? Didn't she just *shine*? The one lucid pebble on the beach speaking its color, with no shame, no distortion. Perhaps, standing there, I expected to sprout wings; to speak in tongues; to silence the begrudgers and the uncomprehending, the takers and the besmirchers, the blamers and the abusers.

Eve covered up in shame. The women in ballooning black down Edgeware Road are gloomy testimony to that—to the danger of the passions. And there *is* danger; I felt it in the bar with the artist that first night and in the panic as the naked photographs began and then progressed. I'd felt it in Mischa's vicious whispered words condensing to water on my cheeks one frenzied, plundered afternoon.

All this time, the Virgin had been hidden in the folds of my story—in the love affairs and earnest attempts at art. Her presence, in pictures and history and feminist deconstruction, told me nothing spiritual, I thought. But she was preparing me. And what she told me then, what she tells me now, as I look back (stumbling on those photos hidden in the back of a wardrobe—still dreaming, years later, of searching for Mischa in labyrinthine buildings) is that my body was made to be a piece of Eden. A piece of that peaceful perfection. *We're made in the image and likeness*, they used to say, and then they said it like it was blah blah blah. Now we don't say it and have even forgotten how to think it.

But imagine a painter sitting down to paint the face of God Almighty—the *is*, the everything—and being able to contemplate nothing but vapor and light. But then this artist finds himself painting a human face with deep eyes, with a long nose, with ears that might ache in the wind, with feet that might sting with blisters from the long walking. Jesus Christ is how God sees himself. Christ is the Icon of God.

We're clothed with flesh in a similar way, and we're icons of the Creator too: dirtied, spoiled—but, through Jesus, utterly redeemable. Our fragile bodies are relics from that garden where we could once walk, whole and unashamed, in the gaze of God and each other. Before it all got complicated.

The truth that I was stumbling toward was that Mary is the most iconic of us all. She is the unsurpassed *solely* human icon— the closest to God. She is *the* Woman. The New Eve, by God's side since the beginning of time.

Really? From the beginning of time?

Ah, but medieval Christians understood this. In monasteries and houses, the prayers of the Divine Office were always echoed by the poor, the uneducated, and the busy, with *Aves* to the Virgin, and by-heart recitation of her Little Office. She was the star they dressed by in the morning and by which sailors navigated the sea. They knew her as the overarching Woman of Scripture who ignites in Genesis and reaches right through to Revelation—the snake-stomper, the conversion-laborer, she who is crowned with twelve stars, clothed with sun, and standing on a crescent moon. They saw her hiding in plain sight in the Psalms, and they sang those songs to her. They knew in their blood that she came before Eve, just as Christ came before Adam. At the beginning of the eternal plan, perfection was already arrived at, and though Mary, in her earthbound life, may not have danced with the Creator of the universe at the dawn of the world, Wisdom did—and, as with so many other things, Christians identified Wisdom with her:

Before the ocean's depths were poured out,
and before there were any glorious fountains
overflowing with water, I was there,
dancing

This girl of Judea is more than one limited mortal by virtue of her essence. What she is, through the grace of God and his plan, stretches from the dawn of time and beyond. She is God's perfected image of innocence, his axis of human Wisdom in the world. She is the image of the Father in its purest yet purely human form. She is uncontaminated and free of association, absolutely untainted by the corrupted gaze of men. And so, to us, then, in London, England, in the twenty-first century, in the steely light of an empty office block in the rain, almost incomprehensible.

For she is a breath of the power of God,
and a pure emanation of the glory of the Almighty;
therefore nothing defiled gains entrance into her.
For she is a reflection of eternal light,
a spotless mirror of the working of God,
and an image of his goodness

Spotless mirror of the working of God. Mary is the entirely human hope that our bodies need not destroy us—that, on the contrary, they link us essentially to the Transcendent. The human body is the way that God expresses himself. (Think of Jesus Christ in his agony on the cross.) And we are made in his image and likeness.

We are made in his image and likeness.

The doors, the doors! In wisdom let us attend

Twenty years later, I would be sitting in a church in Rome as the black-robed Byzantine priest cried these words through clouds of incense before the confession of the Creed. He was keeping out the unchurched, the irreverent, those who don't know, yet, *how* to see. Our eyes can corrupt anything that we look on—even and especially the sacred. And the body is sacred. There is nothing wrong or shameful in the body per se. "The Creator of our bodies knew what he was doing," St. Cyril said. There's nothing wrong with me naked. There's nothing wrong even with *the Mother of God* naked. But I want to yell at the artist who photographed me, at Chris Ofili with his elephant dung: the problem is that *we do not know how to see.*

When, as an avowed atheist, I stepped into that room containing the picture of Mary made out of excrement and cherubim made from pornographic cutouts, I gently fell to pieces. It could not have been that I minded the degradation of the Mother of

God, because for me there was no such thing. It must have been that I was reeling at the sight of *Womankind* so mocked, so humiliated. In Ofili's art, the gaze of the Woman's dissimilar eyes is laden with a wounded hostility. Her swollen nipple and splayed leg are flung in opposite directions. She has no hands! We have come nowhere. We have trashed any modicum of progress. This woman is armless, handless. More than submissive, she is mutilated. This is womanhood beaten to a pulp of ugly incapacity.

There are other naked Madonnas: Edvard Munch painted the Virgin exposed in sexual ecstasy with a red halo. But he, like all the others, misunderstood the sublimity of her form. I see indifference in the eyes of Munch's Madonna, and contempt. The quiddity of true love and ecstasy (the perfect blend of *eros* into *agape*) is clear and arrow-like; it only illuminates. When the substance of pure love is interpreted by the disillusioned, the sad, the hungry, the angry (i.e., most of us), it warps into power games, shame, and hurt. She is powerful, the feminists might say of Munch's Madonna. I say, better to keep her clothes on.

The fact is that no one is ready to see Mary dance naked at the dawn of time. For us, dancing and nakedness segue quickly into the erotic, and the doors open to the stampeding dopamine hits, the snowballing fantasies of concupiscence and pornography. Which means that we are incapable of thinking of the Virgin *dancing*; we are incapable of thinking of her *naked*. We are stooped and narrow-sighted as Adam and Eve lurching out of the Garden. That afternoon in the artist's studio, I was light years from knowing that dancing and nakedness are, in fact, part of the Virgin. He made us naked; he loves us to dance, just as David danced before the tabernacle.

But *holy things for the holy*. We would hardly know what we were looking at if we saw a dancing Madonna, a naked Madonna. We couldn't begin to understand.

The lover's eyes and the artist's eyes are privileged, though. They often try to look on both the nuts and bolts of the physical and the heights of divinity. The lover and the artist should know that they are salvaging pieces of Eden—bodies lost, sometimes ruined, but cast in the image of perfection.

"No one else will ever see you like this," Mischa whispered one day as he looked at me with pure love. He could not risk me being distorted by another gaze. Sad and spoiled, he knew his own purity of heart would only last until he reached his car. "You are her!" Lippi might have crooned to Lucrezia as he finished his painting with sweaty concentration. But Lucrezia, the other side of the canvas, bruises into sin like handled fruit. Mary does not.

After the modeling session, I reached home, cold and wet, and knelt by the gas fire, unsure of what I knew. I looked at my Raphael print of *The Madonna of the Pinks* framed above the mantelpiece. She was still not the true Woman, but was at least more solid and real-looking than other Madonnas. At least she looked as though she were communicating with the world.

I'd almost given up finding an image that spoke of her.

The Newcastle photographer and I had long since parted. I would be forever grateful to him for showing me different ways of seeing. The artist and I never saw each other again. As I walked home from Camden tube nearing my departure from London, I couldn't bear the heavy tread of feet, the thick smell of marijuana, the bass thud from bars, the colors and smells of street food—curry, ginger, cabbage, shish kebab—the herds of wary tourists, the in-your-face beggars, the gangs of boys circling me and daring me to run, or stay. Among the noise and mass of bodies, there was Moira in a long black coat pushing her bicycle toward me up the street. I trotted up to her, but she didn't see me. She still didn't see me when I spoke through the drizzle. I bent to her as close as I dared and spoke again, more loudly: "Hello? Moira?" Her eyes were glassy, unseeing; entirely absorbed in her world—something she was reading, something she heard on the radio. I stepped away without disturbing her.

I walked on and climbed the hill to see London spread out before me with its millions of people, its dancing feet. There was no one up there with me. For long seconds there were no faces at all. Only silence. And birdsong asserting itself on the white air.

Our Lady of Guadalupe,
acheiropoieton, 1531

TWO

Tower

i

Again, one preparing to sail and about to voyage over
raging waves
calls upon a piece of wood more fragile than the ship that
carries him

When, as a child, I read Laura Ingalls Wilder's account of jour-
neying by wagon into the Prairies, one part stayed with me
forever: the endlessness of the horses' hooves beating out form
on the formless ground. They must have sounded like the ticking
of the first clock on time's unchartered infinity. What good the
horses' hooves on an inexhaustibly unchanging landscape? What
good the metronomic ticking when what is marked is uncontrol-
lable and never-ending?

More than a hundred years had passed since that story, but
in many hundreds of square miles on the Midwestern Plains, not
much had changed. Between towns that looked as though they
had been hammered up that afternoon by a film crew, there was
not a ripple in the land, not a house, not a tree, barely a color.
In winter, the landscape was white and empty. In summer, the
grasses were bleached to bone. As drivers approached one of those
flimsy settlements, red, green, and yellow neon signs stuttered
news of tattoo parlors and liquor stores like frantic benedictions.

It was the beginning of a millennium, and even an ultra-
modern society such as this was not capable of contemplating
this fact without unease. Tech experts worked night and day to
ensure that planes didn't fall out of the sky or whirring hospitals flip to darkness. We cringed in communal apprehension, no

matter how in control we thought we were. At the turn of the year 1000, the medievals feared plague, pestilence, the coming of fire and flood. At the turn of the second millennium, our fear was that our technology would kill us. The night of the Virgin birth was written into our consciousness and infrastructure like a timer; deep down it still calibrated everything.

The nothingness of the Plains that surrounded the town I was to live in for a year—to take a break from nursing and to study literature at the local university—was brutally new to me. The flat yellow landscape we drove through on the way from the airport to Jen's house held nothing but the occasional farm. Jen and I sat in expanses of silence through the hour-long ride. We hadn't seen each other since we were children, when she came across the sea on an exchange program to my older brother's class. She had grown into an athletic and serious woman who took her responsibilities toward the younger child that I had been earnestly. Her brown unmade-up eyes turned often and wordlessly to me as she offered me candy and played songs for me on the stereo. I wasn't used to how reticent and polite Americans could be, how empty their land, how confusingly tidy their geometrical streets.

But the house we pulled up to on Magnolia Street was beautifully messy—even in winter. At the corner of a very ordinary Midwestern road, its dead vines and wisteria, which tangled around the railing on the deck, made it seem to belong more to the ghostly South than the Plains. Jen climbed the steps, apologizing for the free newspapers heaped on the path. The grey house's three floors gave the illusion of bending forward over the street (possibly because of the small wooden balcony that jutted out from the attic room), and the windows were like mournful eyes (which I always feel with houses, but in this case seemed especially pronounced). As Jen fumbled with keys, I drifted to the side of the house and saw at the bottom of the long yard the strangest collection of branches tied together. They were arranged to look like a dancer, a child, and a teepee, and were placed equidistantly along the back fence.

Jen peered around the corner to find me.

"C'mon. Snow's on the way."

As I opened my mouth to ask about the branches, she cackled.

"Those are Susan's. You'll like her. You're sharing the second floor."

In fact, it would be many weeks before Susan and I even talked, beyond a review of what was in the fridge and how to silence the phone. (My grandfather sometimes absent-mindedly called from England at 3 a.m.) I knew from what Jen told me that Susan taught at the local high school and had a gnawing aspiration to be an artist. On nights her ten-year-old son wasn't with his father, he joined her in the house on Magnolia Street. On other nights, Bill, a guitarist from Rapid City, was in her room. But in those early days—through quirks of work and class schedules, jetlag and reserve—I rarely saw them, or Jen and her partner Jenny, who lived in the rest of the house.

The snow certainly came, and completed my aloneness, not to mention my nostalgia for the twisted streets of London. I stubbornly attempted to take my daily walk but got no further than the icy corner of the street, and met no one on my way. The only sounds I heard were church bells playing "Eidelweiss" mechanically on the hour. Soon the sidewalks were impassable and the house was filled with crystalline silence.

Now with poetry to write for new classes, I found I could write nothing. The poets' standby—to look around and write what you see—was negated. As far as I was concerned, there was nothing to see. But I knew enough already to know that the core of good poems had little to do with the poet; in a poem, the inspiration, the knotted collection of truth, arrived from all four corners of the globe, the heavens, and the deepest recesses of the unconscious. What mysterious wind collected and bound these pieces for the poet to then prune and arrange I couldn't say, but I was drawn to ritual, to the poetry of the pagan, which I believed to be the natural scaffolding on which Christianity had draped itself. The pagan White Goddess fascinated me, as she had so many poets before me. She was the archetype through which all life was born (the goddess as bride), lived (the goddess as mother), and died (the goddess as crone). I had a vague sense that Mary, as historical woman, had been elevated far beyond her nature to fulfill man's natural desire to worship this goddess. She, as woman of Annunciation, Nativity, and Sorrow, fulfilled all these roles. We had taken her, small woman of Nazareth, blanked out her face in icons, then, in the Renaissance, made her flesh-and-blood expression so utterly remote that she belonged with nothing but the stars. She was distant, blank, a projection screen of what the world wanted, which happened to be male domination.

Earth, divine goddess, Mother Nature . . . began the incantation I would recite before I wrote. These might have been my first spoken prayers, directed to a goddess as I sat at my desk, desperately bargaining for the gift of creation. With her outstretched horizontal wings, Isis seemed a template for the outstretched arms of Christ on the cross. That shape, like a constellation in the shared consciousness of humanity, seemed to have been forged from before the beginning of time. I concluded that Christians had stolen Isis' more ancient form. I also, with disappointment, noted that even the great Isis was often depicted with her divine son Horus; even she was that very ordinary thing: a *mother.* Yet, perhaps because of the unreal nature of the drawings of her, Isis seemed imbued with power. *Earth, divine goddess, Mother Nature,* the ancient prayer to her began, *who dost generate all things and bringest forth ever anew the sun.* Staring at the clean lines of her feathered wings, I wanted only to conjure poetry that, I felt, could somehow save my story. Mary's story of motherhood and loss seemed too small to be of any use to me—too human and too sad.

It took spring to unlock my new life on the Plains to me. With the coming of the milder weather, a meter-long icicle fell from the balcony of the house, coneflowers bloomed in the lanes, and the air softened and rippled like candleflames. The warmer weather brought Susan out of her room too. She stumbled past me one day, a hammer and saw in her hands, her pale little face intent on holding a screwdriver between her lips, her taupe-colored hair pinned up to clear the way for her labors. On my rambles along the lilac-bordered backstreets, there were so few cars around that Susan's hammering and chopping could be heard blocks away. On weekends, she sketched or nailed together her strange creations in the yard or performed her laborious yoga moves on the deck, and her careless warmth and offhand interest in whatever I was doing swept me toward her—like the many cats, bats, and snakes she befriended and wouldn't let any of us trap or shoo away. There was no gradual gear-change in our friendship: what had been so quiet and withheld on the second floor through winter seemed to explode in spring to full-on confidences and hilarious evenings drinking wine. Once the week had come to an end, she became my go-to person to tell my tales about classes and college friends—and to lament to when missing London crept up on me. "You're not missing it," she'd say as she sketched. "You're just someone destined to have a foot in two places."

The other inhabitants of 918 Magnolia Street, Jen and Jenny, were also more visible in the warmer weather, although they both, in their different ways, had kept an eye on me through the snows. Jenny, a cozy-looking accountant who sometimes had a hard time understanding what I said, changed my car oil, cooked the rare hot meals I sat down to eat, and often (I'm ashamed to say) did my laundry. Jen, rake-thin and ever-watchful of me, left encouraging notes on my breakfast plate and drove me to ball games at weekends.

In the new warmth, we began to grill together in the yard once a week. We would discuss our troubles and eulogize a life without men. At nightfall, once the air was cold, we snuggled under blankets, dissected our pasts, told each other we deserved better, and generally felt we were all on the verge of brilliant futures.

In the shelter of this community of women, I finally began to write. "The love of form," writes the poet Louise Gluck, "is a love of endings." The Plains represented a constant search for form; for a poet, I suppose it was this that began to make them irresistible. The long run of land I confronted when I drove out to the store began to look like a long drink of freedom: sometimes I purposely missed the turning for the mall and just kept driving. The landscape's seductive austerity, mixed with Ezra Pound's exhortation to a similar poetic asceticism, formed me. *This stillness,* I wrote as I felt that stillness quiver into life, *ricochets sounds like a drum. The snow hisses like sand, shifts with nothing to stop it.*

I didn't consciously seek Mary. It must have been around that time, though, that I came across a Midwestern Madonna in the university library. I'd taken to finding peace there between classes, in the art section where no one seemed to go. The book was open at a table, and at first I thought it was a historical portrait of just any woman—and perhaps it was. In 1921, William Henry Dethlef Koerner painted his *Madonna of the Prairie* in modest, Victorian dress seated on a wagon and slackly holding the reins. The woman's posture in the picture is generally slack; she slouches, and her expression is passive, even hopeless—or childlike. She seems fazed by the barren eternity ahead of her. But she is pretty, in a European drawing room kind of way, and the cover of the wagon frames her like a halo. The space around her head is the light of the halo; the folds of the wagon covering are like wrinkled skin—but also reminiscent, I would later think, of the thin darts of light that frame the 1531 Guadalupe apparition of the Virgin. What Mary lacks in Koerner's vision is transcendence: his Madonna is stubbornly human, despite the suggestion of a halo. She is all thinking about the beans she has to cook, the crushing fatigue of heat and small children. She is one of us; she has no power. And if there was no power, it seemed to me, what was the point?

Jen's mother, who knew my old fascination with Marian art, dropped by with one other image of Mary that spring: an American-Indian Madonna with her child in a papoose. I taped it to my wall, but, equally, I knew she wasn't Mary; this woman was beautiful, powerful, and proud (and somehow, even then, I knew that this kind of power, and pride, did not belong with Mary). In any case, I was tired of always seeing the Virgin with her child. I had no general interest in children, and every woman I knew in the state was either divorced or gay. Susan's lover was still around, but I never saw him. There was her son, Joe, but he drifted independently (in what seemed to me a utopian way) between his parents' houses. More usually, the narrative of motherhood seemed a blocking one. It implied an unnegotiable relationship with men. And after my tethered devotion to Mischa and my failure at intimacy with the photographer, I had had it with men. Only a couple approached me that year. One, a fellow student, asked if I'd seen the abandoned farmhouses out on the Plains. Would I like to go with him to smash one up? He had a gun. We could shoot out windows. I spent the rest of the year avoiding him. The other, a cowboy with brown eyes, saw me reading Emily Dickinson in a coffeeshop, drove me home, and kissed me memorably. But afterward, I ignored his calls.

At the end of May, Jen and Jenny took off for Mexico, and Susan went to stay in New York with her sister. That summer, through tornado sirens and increasing heat, I spent hours on the creaky internet reading about Our Lady of Guadalupe. Why I did, I cannot for the life of me recall, except that I was always looking for material for poems, and this was a story filled with unexpected blooming and female power (as I perceived it), and I was increasingly obsessed with the notion of something transcendent that did not seem too attached to organized religion.

So I wrote poems about the Mexican peasant Juan Diego and his walk on which he met the mysterious woman in the star-covered cloak on the hill of Tepeyac. I loved that she spoke to him in his own Nahuatl, and that she sent him up the barren winter hill to find miraculous Castilian roses. I loved the cosmological, otherworldly appearance of this Madonna with all her signs, which was so unlike Fra Lippi's fleshy maiden. Yet, still, this Mary that I scrutinized on the computer screen would not look up. I couldn't understand why she would not look up.

When Susan returned from New York, we had the house to ourselves and became closer than ever. One day, we drove out to Omaha for lunch and to poke around the flea market. She was always looking for objects for her art—this time, ostrich eggs and semiprecious jewels. Even as she drove, her small grey eyes seemed to be listening to something far away, inventing and designing. But she always pressed me for what I thought, what I was doing. As the flat land ran endlessly by us, life seemed to shimmer with possibilities.

In the flea market, Susan never found her ostrich egg—only a handful of costume jewelry. But there, among yellow-spotted books and flappers' bling and feathers, I lighted on a small wooden sculpture of Mary. As with Lippi's painting of Lucrezia, it was the simplicity of the piece that pulled me in, the clear lines. The carving was absolutely symmetrical and unadorned: she was standing, tiny feet and hands together, praying, the long sleeves of her robe tapering her shape like a petal. We look for order and form in art—a taming and transformation of chaos that peaks in the rose window at Chartres, the tightly structured beauty of Dante's paradise—and the Virgin, in that piece, seemed like a precise part of an immense and glorious design.

"You should have her," Susan whispered at my elbow. "You're a Mary person, I guess."

I bought the figurine and would keep it on my desk through the decades and countries that followed.

The days continued, long and full of poetry—Berryman, Stevens, Ginsberg, Whitman, Dickinson. Sometimes I would put Susan's son, Joe, to bed when he was staying over and read him *Harry Potter* before lights out. On the way back to his father's in the morning, we sauntered the back alleys of town searching for kittens he'd seen in someone's yard till we were both hopelessly lost and late. During that summer, for the first time in my life (and actually the last), I fell into any bed where I found myself at the end of the day and slept easily. If we were talking late, I bunked up with Susan, whose bed smelt of wood shavings and musky rose. If I were watching a late movie with Jen and Jenny, they would cover me with a blanket as I fell asleep on their couch. If I were reading to Joe, I might fall asleep beside him. If I happened to wake and walk barefoot through the front door and downtown on the still-warm road in full moonlight, there was no one to call me back or call me crazy.

It must have been September when I began to wonder how I would ever go back to London. I was sitting with Jen and Jenny in the yard reading Emerson ("I must be myself. I cannot break myself any longer for you, or you. If you can love me for what I am, we shall be happier. If you cannot, I will still seek to deserve that you should. I must be myself. I will not hide my tastes or aversions. I will so trust that what is deep is holy, that I will do strongly before the sun and moon whatever inly rejoices me and the heart appoints") and wondering what to eat for supper when I had the thought that I had never been happier in my life.

And then, long before I was ready, winter came again.

ii

I carried him who carries earth and sky
and yet am still a maid

No one was around that night as I drove home after class in the darkness. Every sound hit snow and ricocheted into air, was held, protected and glittering, in the white stillness. The house was chilly. Jen and Jenny were staying in Omaha for the weekend. I found Susan doing yoga in three sweaters and a scarf, and went through to the kitchen to let her finish up. There were fried eggs left over from breakfast on the stove, and the coffee was gritty and stale. I opened a bottle of red wine and started to drink. The Eden of our summer had disintegrated. Susan and I both knew that we were facing ragged and uncertain futures. Alone and jobless, I didn't want to go home to London. As the day of my flight approached, I was unprepared. I had done none of the job of leaving a place: the many small goodbyes that have to be said; the many closings of doors; the shaking of hands; the orderly, necessary regret; the packing. My sadness at leaving the student life was sunk so deep in my head that it was like a death I'd denied. Susan hated her job. The snow kept her indoors and hid her growing sculpture park. Her relationship with the guitarist had stuttered out. I knew her heart was not exactly broken; I also knew that despite her absorption in yoga and art, she hated being on her own. Celibacy was, for her, a truncation of what she could be, a kind of bloodless living.

There was a glorious bunch of red roses on the draining board, ribbon and a pair of scissors. I knew what Susan had in mind. For both of us, occult dabblings were mere extensions of our emotions; we needed physicality and gesture. In the face of loss and desperation, we needed to *do*. And never had it been so easy. Witchery really meant nothing more than harnessing our own power and Mother Nature. I had been given one of those glittery collections of spells as a leaving gift from a friend in London and loved the folklorish rituals. The book was propped open at a page on the table.

Susan came into the kitchen holding up a black-and-white photo of me that one of our photographer friends had taken. In the picture I had two grainy faces, like the Egyptian goddess Bat: "I am praise, I am majesty, I am Bat with her two faces, I am the one who is saved, and I have saved myself from all things evil."

"Look at you. I asked for a copy to keep you with me when you've gone," she grinned sadly, pinning the photo to the wall and putting her hair up. I had never seen her pale face so clearly: it had the stubborn, painful expectancy of a child on a rainy morning. Then, "We need to do a spell to bring me a new lover and a new job that doesn't involve teaching. And for your future. Whatever it is you want."

Whatever it was I wanted. One professor suggested I might like to stay on in the US and do a PhD. Shocked as I was at the prospect of leaving the Plains, I think I simply lacked the courage to stay away from what I saw as the center of the world. But anyone who has ever faced leaving a place where they have lived intensely for a finite period of time will recognize my heartbrokenness.

I watched Susan cut a lock of her long hair.

"You need to cut the roses exactly in half. Use that knife by the coffee machine; it's sharper."

It always amazed me how focused and practical Susan could become when it came to art and magic.

I found the knife but hesitated as I stood before the vivid red of the blooms. On the prairies in December, the roses were as unlikely as the ones that Juan Diego came upon on Tepeyac Hill that January in 1531.

"They must have cost you a fortune."

"If it doesn't cost, it's not a sacrifice," Susan grinned again.

I sunk the blade. There was something very satisfying about slicing the succulent petals—like Abraham, I would think years later when I began to read the Old Testament, halving his sacrifices of a heifer, a goat, and a ram, but bloodless.

I cut a lock of my own hair and we arranged it, and Susan's, between the rose halves and tied them together with ribbons.

"Now," she consulted the book, "we have to throw them into running water with an incantation."

"There is no running water."

"What about a faucet?"

I looked at the sparkly book she was reading from. "It should be a naturally occurring source of water."

"What about the fountain on campus? Would that count?"

"It's frozen."

"What about the creek?"

"Frozen too."

"Yes, but under the ice, the water's still running. The creek's running under the ice. If we throw the roses on now, when the thaw comes they'll be taken anyway. It'll be a slow-motion spell."

She was already flying upstairs to get Joe out of bed. His dad was stuck in Pierre in the snow.

Outside was even more silent than when I arrived. We wrapped Joe in a blanket over his pajamas, ski jacket, and boots, and tucked him in the back of the car. He had a lot of questions as we drove down to the bluff, but he was used to our bizarre ideas.

By the frozen creek, the bare trees were pale and majestic against the black sky. Not a bird flew, not a car drove by. It was as still and deep as prayer.

"What do we say?"

Susan stared at the book in her gloved hands and began to read, her voice muffled by her scarf.

What power did we think we were harnessing? I wondered about offloading my giant grief at leaving the Plains onto the frozen waters. I wondered if Susan really believed that our shenanigans that night would bring her a soulmate. We thought we could solve reality through the power of symbol and visualization, through the seasons and the imagery of flowers. Did we really believe in an omnipotent goddess? There was some elemental need in us for a divine being, and it had to be feminine. This female power was more ancient (I felt) than the patriarchal religions, which were (I believed) all about oppression.

Is it possible that the Virgin was there by that frozen river, hiding in a tree? That God willed her to listen? It seemed impossible that there was no supernatural presence: the very ground seemed to need it.

But there was only whiteness, a killing stillness.

"You have to toss the flowers onto water, right?" Joe squeaked. "There's just ice!"

"Under the ice the water's still running. Slowly, but it's still running," Susan murmured.

"Don't we have to do something else? It doesn't seem like it's enough," I forced out through numb lips. "Shouldn't we slay a deer or something?" I was joking, but it did seem that some kind of blood offering would make this more efficacious.

"I don't see you slaying a creature," Susan said witheringly.

"Bring us lovers and futures worthy of us," she called over the ice with finality, and we flung our roses.

The stars were harder and brighter than I had ever seen them. After Abraham's sacrifices, a deep and terrifying darkness descended on him. In the sky's black silence, I almost heard acknowledgment of our futility; the roses fell with anti-climactic little thuds.

"I love you both!" Joe yelled, as if he sensed an answer was called for, and we laughed and shivered our way back to the car.

იი

December arrived. There were two more weeks till my departure for London, and I was, unexpectedly, on my way to a winter wedding. Snow had fallen heavily again, but the plows had gone through, and the drive to the big city was tinged with lilac stillness. Elaine, an assistant professor in the English department, drove me. She was glamorous in a wry, intellectual way, with long curly hair and huge earrings, and had taken me under her wing through the year, explaining department dynamics (*"Please—* they're sleeping together") and acting as my agent in the face of innumerable invitations and squabbling over who got to host me. ("She's seen the Black Hills. If you wanna do a good thing, take her to the Badlands, why don't you?" "I don't think she needs to see a rodeo; she can get that at Disney." "The book club wants a talk from you, and so does the hospital. Why? I don't know. I'll see if I can get them to pay you . . .") Elaine had plenty to say about the marriage we'd be attending, and we spent the journey out there going through the whys and wherefores and worrying (in the most superficial and entertaining sense) how it might end.

It was unlike any wedding I'd been to. The Spanish bride's white dress was the size of a small hot air balloon, the building was carpeted and toasty, the ceremony took three minutes, and the glasses of gin and lime kept coming. The groom was Slovenian, and the whole occasion had a sense of rootlessness and the sparkle of giftwrap and ice. There was no family from Europe there, just people from the English department, all dolled up and avidly enjoying the appetizers and free alcohol.

It was that night I met a woman who, like a wind, would skew those last days entirely in her own direction. She was called Marianne, Elaine said, as the tall woman across the room stared at me and strode over. "She's miss popular, is what she is . . ."

In a long grey dress, her dark hair short and messy, Marianne descended on me like the answer to a spell, fixed me with her very grey eyes, and guessed my star sign and my favorite poem. As I stood there in my red velvet dress, clutching my gin, the rest of the room, including Elaine, became faceless and small. Marianne led me by the hand to a chair at her table and told me I should—I *would*—stay in the States.

Cancer had kept Marianne away from her job at the university all the time that I was there, but through the year I'd heard tell of her from many people and had already concluded that she was the kind to inspire infatuations: too many people told me, with a dazed look in their eyes, that I *had* to meet her. I even remember being grateful, as I passed her closed office door, that our paths never crossed. That year was all about reclaiming power; love only took that away.

Marianne certainly had power, though she possibly didn't know it. She seemed to be at the head of the table that night, though the table was round, and—in a breath-stopping, all-consuming way—only had time for me. Her skin was sallow, her jaw and cheekbones like carved rock, but her voice was breathy as a 1950s starlet. She smiled at me constantly, as if I bewitched her, and told me I must stay with her in her guestroom in the next town; I couldn't leave. She had heard me at a college poetry reading, and she wanted to hear more of my poems; she wanted them handwritten on her walls, to carry them in her purse, to have them tattooed on her skin. I remembered the reading she talked about but could not remember seeing her there. All year I had experienced the frisson of being different and temporary. It was clear to people that they couldn't ask much of me, that I was both foreign and fleeting, and because of that I was often regarded with a kind of wistful longing. But Marianne was lining up drinks for me in homage. She was shushing people if they tried to join our conversation. As I tackled my third gin and lime, I spied the bride and groom make their underwhelming departure from the hotel lobby from the corner of my eye. It became a night of booze and lucky guesses, a night when you find connections with a person and slot life into life—my love of Yeats into yours, your red wine into my glass, your thoughts about *écriture féminine* into what I wrote in my notebook last year, these lines I can quote into the next two lines you can quote; what you say sits right with me, slays me, I have to write it down; we can't sleep until we've shared every detail of our lives.

We talked and drank until the last grad student had reluctantly drained his final beer and the waiters were putting on the overhead lights, and I knew I had to go home with the sober Elaine, who was lurking impatiently in the foyer. Marianne followed me sadly out to the big revolving door, took off one of her crimson glass earrings, and pressed it into my hand. It matched my dress. Conscious of my gin-soaked words leaning heavily on each other, I told her I'd wear it on a string around my neck.

"If you're really going, we have to spend every moment together till then."

Elaine glared at me when she heard that, and all the ride home I fought off her analysis and questions. I didn't want to prune what had happened down to words. Not now. Maybe never.

It's a measure of my madness that in those days I thought only of seeing Marianne. I skipped commencement and spent almost no time at home. I neglected Susan, Jen, and Jenny. I wondered about calling Marianne, but twice, when the phone was in my hands, I hung up. When I finally left her a message and received no reply, I felt physically dizzy. My last days in the States were disappearing before my eyes.

Even then, I interrogated this awful hunger (as did Susan, Jen, and Jenny, who were mildly hurt, and certainly agog). Was this my first lesbian love affair? Was this a natural progression in the all-female world in which I found myself? After my history of dating in London, I had nothing much left but disdain for the opposite sex and was often called out for my man-hating remarks by men in my classes. But much as I would have loved to embrace an all-female world, I could conjure no sexual need for Marianne. There was no moral imperative I needed to consider. Emotion of the strength that I was experiencing in those days would, yes, often be resolved in a physical act. I reasoned that intense feeling had to be transformed, like rain into ice, if certain conditions were present—like desperation, longing, and not knowing what else to do. This was my sexual creed at the beginning of the new century.

But my feelings for Marianne weren't like that. There was only this longing to sit near her, to be by her. *I feel like I'm driving fast down a road and the road just ran out, but I can't stop*, I wrote to her. *Come over*, she wrote back finally, with dozens of excuses for her silence. But then the blizzard came.

It took down email and phones. A white hand flattened the town's every detail and insisted overwhelmingly that everyone stay where they were, with whom they happened to be. I paced the house like a woman in solitary confinement, my suitcases still empty, my goodbyes and thankyous unsaid. I could only pick up the phone compulsively and listen to its disconnected hiss. Look at the windows like blind white eyes. "Stay inside, stay safe," the cheery newsreader advised.

"You're trying to hold onto the Plains. Or this year. But your hands are too small," Susan said sadly when she found me sitting in front of the blank computer screen. I knew she was right. I held onto Susan's hand and felt the beginnings of ordinary grief swell in my throat. But then, an email came from the woman herself: *I like this weather, actually. It reminds us we're not in charge.*

I could have shaken her.

That evening, when the blizzard had settled to ground level, I quietly packed the car with blankets, candles, matches, and a bottle of wine, and set off. Jen and Jenny were stuck out of town at Jenny's parents, Susan was taking a long hot bath, and Joe was with his father. There were no hands to pull me back. As I turned onto the highway, it became apparent that only one lane was passable. My headlights lit a swirl of powdery snow across it, and I could see no further than two feet in front of me. Still, I thought, two feet at a time, two feet at a time. Of course, I knew that if the car broke down, I would freeze to death within half an hour, and no one else was likely to pass by to help me. There were no cell phones. Into my head leapt the image of pioneer women who walked out on nights like these, or nights of dust and tornado, incapable of living a moment longer in those elements. Then, as I drove, other images came in the whiteness of memory: hikers I had read about, frozen to death on the side of the road, faces and fingers eaten by ice.

By this point it was impossible for me to turn around. I couldn't tell if I was on the road or drifting into a ditch. I wondered how close I was to one of the couple of farms that broke that stretch of highway. I also wondered, as I crawled along at twenty miles per hour, if I'd survive the walk from my car to any such front door. I thought, for the first time in a long time, of how scared I had been just to come here: the evenings I spent sitting in my flat in London thinking about the wagon ride that Laura Ingalls Wilder took into the prairies, the profound panic of the limitless space. The danger of nothing. That nothing muffled me now, and an animal instinct for survival gave me a reluctant kick of fear. There were no lights but my own headlights, and they lit nothing but a fistful of whirling snow. I didn't know how to stay on the road or how much more road there was, but stopping meant freezing to death.

Many years later, I would have a dream colored by that lethal night. By then I would be living in Italy, and the road in the dream led down to the Tyrrhenian Sea, but there was deep snow in the dream too, and darkness. I was in a car, and as I approached a crossing by a church, one hundred yards from the water, my brakes failed on the ice and my headlights were spent. I had to make a choice to surrender, to let myself be carried over the crossing toward the water in darkness, to blindly give assent. It was a gift of a dream: a brief encapsulation of the Dark Night—the purgation of the old self, the letting go of will, fear, and memory. So many stories begin with those words, *On a dark night*. It's the precursor of any change. The dream was dark but held no fear. It came just after my newfound belief in God.

On the Plains a decade before that dream, I was also taken forward on ice, but in godless panic. I thought of the halved roses Susan and I had hurled onto the creek, the mooted blood sacrifice.

In such a situation, anyone might have prayed. In the face of floods, tornadoes, fire, and blizzard, people do pray—even those who don't believe. Because sometimes it's all there is to do. When there is no human remedy, prayer is our first course of action. In the desert of hopelessness, it's our first act of creation. In the abyss that we sing of in the Psalms, we're wired to find *something*. And in every culture since the dawn of time, we've looked to the skies. In the unchartered space between Bethel and Ai, Abram built an altar to the one God. In Hebron by the oaks, he built another. Outside the city of Shechem, Jacob built another. Wherever men stumble in exile and nothingness, they build a place to sacrifice and speak to God. I would come to know in my bones why they did this when I became a believer because that night is written into me as a blank canvas for meeting with God.

But I had yet to learn that prayer is what we grasp when we lack any coordinate. I had yet to learn that, as the closest person to him, filled with grace as a glass is filled with water, the Virgin *is* prayer. *Give me a drink*, we might say, grasping a glass of water. *Let us pray*, we say, taking hold of Mary's hand. I was before all this; there was no hand, no prayer.

Years later, I would hear them call Mary the Tower of David in their litanies of mixed metaphor. This was as incomprehensible to me as the bride's teeth being like a flock of ewes in Solomon's Song. And, I wondered, how can she be, simultaneously, the New Eve, the gate, the star, and also a tower? But I see now, looking back at myself as I blindly crossed that flat land, she *is* a tower. A tower (something so totally lacking on the Plains, which have no landmark, no reference, no haven) has deep foundations, and it goes way up into the sky. It links earth and heaven. It's a break in the earth's horizontal narrative of despair. It's the breath of the long-distance swimmer, the tether for the floating astronaut. When they call the Virgin a tower, what they're saying is that she is a living prayer, rising up in the wilderness. In blazing sun, she offers the shade of God; in storms, she gives shelter.

The Lord is thy keeper, the pioneers read on the Sabbath, *the Lord is thy shade upon thy right hand. The sun shall not smite thee by day, nor the moon by night.*

How quickly those pioneers must have run to the shelter of their prayers! There, in the snow, I couldn't see God; I couldn't see that Tower of David, Mary. The goddess that Susan and I summoned was, suddenly, irrelevant. What strange and paltry sacrifices we thought she asked of us, and with no answering sacrifice from the sky, no bleeding God to suffer with us. Those pagan prayers slipped from me like a slack handshake.

Like Juan Diego when he tried to avoid the Virgin as he hastened to find a priest for his sick uncle, I was avoiding (unconsciously) turning to this woman I had gazed at in so many paintings on so many walls. I might otherwise have spoken to *la mestiza* who had walked with me so strangely all summer. From the image that was revealed on Juan Diego's cloak as it poured forth those miraculous gathered roses, I recognized her as a woman of queenliness, even connected to godliness, but one firmly rooted in the complex human form. The stooped shape of La Guadalupe seemed to sum up every dilemma: an ordinary woman of two races, both marginalized and conquering, who unfolded to shelter the entire stumbling world: "Am I not here who am your Mother? Are you not under my shadow and protection? Am I not the source of your joy? Are you not in the hollow of my mantle, the crossing of my arms?"

The painting of La Guadalupe, I did not know it then, is an *acheiropoieton*: the image appeared on Juan Diego's cloak apparently through no human contrivance. There was no love-sick friar behind it, no Renaissance master. It came as if from nowhere. This Mary has swollen eyes, her head is bent, her hands are carefully praying, one knee is raised slightly as if to dance. Her cloak of stars is like the sky, her Aztec belt says she is pregnant, her loose hair says she is a virgin. In the folds of her dress is the sacrifice, the sacrificial bleeding lamb that will cancel forever the obliterating whiteness of the snow. She is raised, yet she bends. She dances, yet she is still. She is looking down, I realize now, at us.

But, my word, I couldn't turn to her that night. I could not tolerate a male God—and Mary, I suspected this much, was inextricable from *him*. My world was populated by women; men were the enemy—the takers, controllers, deceivers. That night, if my car had broken down and a man had stopped to help me, I would have assumed he intended rape or kidnap.

I was already wedded to a rational explanation of Mary's story and assumed she was a victim of rape: it was one of the narratives I was toying with to explain the conception of the Messiah. I was making notes on new poems that would flesh out what I thought must have happened at the Annunciation: abuse, or a secret love affair. I thought that she, like me, was at the mercy of her own passions, or the passions of men. The mother, Mary of Nazareth, had to be the embodiment of powerlessness. She was too tied up with the other sex for it to have been otherwise. "For the first time in human history the mother kneels before her son," Simone de Beauvoir wrote of the Virgin. "She freely accepts her inferiority. This is the supreme masculine victory, consummated in the cult of the Virgin—it is the rehabilitation of woman through the accomplishment of her defeat."

How could I ever have turned to her on that snow-blind drive when this was what I believed? Disillusioned with men, and disappointed in the new place of women in the world, which seemed to want us only to be more like men, we turned to many-faced, many-named, many-handed goddesses. We wanted what the world sees as freedom and power, but the more we stretched out our hands for those things, the more the world seemed to mock women's strange predilection to serve children and God. So we didn't serve them. And our womanhood was robbed.

Decades on, there are now a tide of young women (puzzled by what it is that makes them women) who are, on the contrary, intent on becoming men. Like Reformation iconoclasts who gouged out the face of Mary in English churches, smashed her statues, and erased her presence from the core of religious devotion, girls will let medics take scalpels to their breasts. Even washing their bodies will make some cry with disgust and despair. They cannot bear to see the form of their own curves; the texture repulses them. They will see Ofili's Madonna in elephant dung, the empty shrines in ancient churches, and, at some incalculable level, they will know what the world thinks of *women*.

For we have long forgotten Wisdom dancing at the dawn of time.

"My soul magnifies the Lord," Mary sang at the accomplishment of what she was made to be. It's clear to me now that in her whole and jubilant womanhood, *she* would never want to be separated from *him*. And for those who say Mary is *sexless*, I say: think of to whom she gives her sexuality and of what else she gives him (her everything); think of how she yielded in her extraordinary conception, of how she loves. In her, there is no division, no rupture, no forgetting of what she is, no self-hatred. There is no falsity, no playacting, no confusion, no withholding from her Maker. She is as responsive as the sea to light and cloud, as generous as air that endlessly expands, as ecstatic as a bride and as faithful. I believe she loves her naked body and is at ease with her breasts and her rounded belly, because he does, and because he is.

Of course she knelt before him.

For what mother, I ask de Beauvoir twenty years after that blizzard, does not kneel before her baby? What mother has not knelt before the crib and felt something like the wordless and surging adoration of prayer? A mother's love for her baby is overwhelming. It crescendos in waves. It comes like labor pains: just as she thinks that she can take no more, the intensity disperses, leaving her gasping. God knows that we can't hold the entirety of love (or pain) in one go. It would tear us to pieces. But mothers have a privileged glimpse of this infinite love that binds us so thoroughly to our children. When we kneel before our child, we are bowing at a glimpse of divine love that effortlessly holds everything.

Mary was effaced that night as I drove through the white. She was always hidden, small—yet utterly bonded to her son. In few scriptural words, we know how she searched for him; how she stood at the window, asking for him; how she was at the wedding, telling him; how she waited under the cross, doing what none of us want to begin to fathom. I could not ever have had Mary without Jesus—nor him without her. She is tightly bound to him even when she is far from him, just as ordinary mothers may be far away from their grown-up children yet carry them always in the dream-sharing warmth of their bodies.

One friend, Sofia, knows this mysterious bond between mother and child better than most. Sofia lost her mother suddenly at the age of eleven and went on to have four children of her own. She said that although, by any rational measure, she has known some of her children for longer than others, it doesn't feel that way. The moment each baby arrived, she said, it felt as if they had been around as long as their siblings, just as the fabric of her relationship with her own long-gone mother sustains: "There must be something that lies outside of time in the bond between a mother and a child." Mothers share this with the divine. God exists both inside and outside of time. He is in the minutes, the hours, and the days, and he is outside them, just like the tie between mother and child. Mothers, in their enhanced capacity to experience infinite love, know something of God's ever-present "now," where one moment is laid on another like layers of transparent paper—like in Leonardo da Vinci's charcoal drawing of a grown Mary sitting on her mother's knee as she, in turn, holds the Christ child. Da Vinci knew the immortality of maternal love. Mary will always be at Anne's knee, even as she nurses her own child. These are the moments we sense when we kneel before our children and gasp with wonder at the eternity of love we cannot possibly experience in one go. Anne knew this. Mary knew this better than any mother. Simone de Beauvoir, perhaps, did not.

When I think of moments as ever-present, of the mother's love out-of-time, I wonder if Mary was already praying for me that night. I wonder if, as her daughter, I was already given to her heart.

There was nowhere to go but the two feet of road in front of me, and the snow dancing in the headlights. But it couldn't have been many minutes before a truck passed me, its two red tail lights the only visible things in the whole white night. I latched onto them, gratefully, closely, all the way into town, conscious of snow spinning on the ground beneath me like clouds, and the path on the highway coming clear by the sheer weight of the truck ahead. I drove, not even wondering anymore why I was making this trip or what it could mean.

Finally, I pulled off the highway and down a street-lit road piled high with drifts on either side. Outside Marianne's house, I grabbed wine from the back seat and hastened up the path. But before I could ring the bell, the bottle slipped through my gloves and broke on the ice. Wine galloped across snow, staining it a deeply satisfying blood-red. Every possible scent was unleashed: wood, blackberry, grape, musk, citrus. This heat against the snow was something like the sacrifice I'd wanted Susan to make back at the creek. I cried out to no one, and rang the bell.

☙

Marianne seemed unconscious of the odyssey I had gone through to get there. I could hear her humming as she strolled down the hallway to open the front door. She hugged me warmly, waved to the notion of the broken bottle on the path, and began putting cookies on a plate in the kitchen as I fell onto the couch and looked around me. As if I had stepped in from a city street in spring, she was telling me about the house, how she had moved there at the beginning of her illness to be nearer to her family.

She hadn't noticed I could barely speak. But in any case, I was more than happy to just listen.

I knew that she was famous in that frozen world, like the whole of her Irish clan. For many years, her father owned a bar on Main Street and her mother taught at the local high school. Her many brothers owned tack stores and stables throughout the county. She was the eldest and the strangest (it seemed to me)—the only one hooked on the literature of her ancestors and disinclined to hunt or fish. Her new house was unlike any other in that part of the state. Everything inside was white or cream, from the sofa to the drapes to the painted table. Yet it wasn't fashionable or expensive looking. You could tell the furniture had been found in junk stores and hastily painted. Glass prisms hung at the window. Glass vases held baby's breath and honesty.

"Do you want a hot bath to warm up?" she called from the kitchen. I peered into the bathroom to find the tub already filled with cold water. I could hear her laughing.

Color and darkness, she said casually as she put a blanket around my shoulders, made her nauseous during her chemotherapy. Her grown-up daughters cleared out anything that wasn't white or transparent to create as much light as possible. Bathwater calmed her. I realized that the house was full of mirrors, water, prisms. Wherever you looked, you were looking at something else.

Maybe it was my youth that made me neglect any real consideration of Marianne's illness, but I could see her fragility now. In fact, she looked plain tired. After my death-defying trip, I was simply worried that I was keeping her up. But I didn't want to leave, even if I could have. I couldn't go back to Susan and the empty suitcases. There were glimmers of Marianne's adoration from the night of the wedding, the old weather, the grabbing me by the hands and saying "Don't go. Get a job here." And I wondered if I really would.

In the dim kitchen we drank wine, giggled, and chaotically tried to recount our entire life stories as we promised each other we would the night of the wedding. She told me of her marriage to Pat when she was seventeen, how she fell for him because of his blue eyes, and how she was divorced at forty. She told me of her teaching jobs and her studies, her friends and her attempts to write a book, her love of heels and her inability to walk in them. She coughed a lot because the radiation had burnt her right lung. But she was *well*, she kept saying. She beat the cancer, she nodded in disbelief. She was alone, she went on with the same stunned look in her eyes, because her lover, Dan, had left her.

There was no order to the talking and no lining up of facts in order of importance. That she preferred red to white wine was given the same emphasis and time as the fact she had just finished radiation therapy. That her cat was called Maud was the same sized fact as Dan walking out.

As a candle spat and the cat woke and jumped up onto the table, she told me she was Catholic—though how large or real that fact was I couldn't know. As a nonbelieving Londoner, I viewed it as I did the Judaism of my Jewish friends—a genetic quirk, a shade in someone's story and humor. She said that being Catholic made her understand poetry and that she knew my poems were *real*. And I, at that age, believed her and thought it meant that I was real too.

"By his bruises we are healed," she said more than once, and I wondered if the line was from T.S. Eliot. "I can't escape the idea of God," she said almost apologetically. "Mom used to say faith gets educated out of a person. Which is pretty bad publicity for religion. And for education, for that matter."

There are people who make you feel as though you are the only person in the world. She wasn't one of them. She made you feel that once she had taken a seat, once she had finished her chores, once she had graded all her papers, once the world had stopped, there would only be you. That moment, I think I knew even then, would never come. Yet her character was filled with that promise: that even if you were not fully bestowed with the gift of her attention, perhaps you would be soon. It was somehow worth hankering after.

She kept getting up and putting things in drawers, or finding pages she wanted to read to me, and saying, "Thank God now I can just sit with you." But she couldn't sit. Soon we were walking back out in the unbelievable cold.

The fall of snow had slowed but kept coming. Dry flakes coated our shoulders and flattened out the sidewalks. Still no cars. I had no idea if I was walking in the road or which way I was headed. We just walked, arm in arm, chins tucked into our collars, heads bent against the wind, through streets with muted lights, and past small houses with no decks, and sad looking plastic Santas and snowmen sticky with ice, and chains of colored electric lights fallen down from crooked eaves. On the sidewalk, a doll's carriage was heaped with snow, and a doll lay face down on the ground. In one yard, a man in a T-shirt shouted obscenities at us through a tinsel-strung fence.

We arrived at a bar on Main Street, where we were interrupted every two minutes by students or relations, all wanting, it seemed to me, to take a piece of Marianne, to be in the peace of that colorless light.

It was a light that would haunt me for decades. Perhaps it was because I wanted to be there forever. I knew my goodbyes would never be said. Elaine, to this day, must be waiting for me to walk into her office. Jen and Jenny probably never remade my bed. I was already dizzy with missing the Plains.

"We will have proper time before you leave, won't we?" Marianne kept saying, holding onto my hands as drinks were sent our way from the bar, and another cousin, a young man with wire-rimmed glasses and a stammer wanting help with a college paper, was dismissed because we had so little time. In a newspaper on our table was a photograph of a man's frostbitten hands. He'd broken down on the same highway I'd driven on and lost three fingers. The remaining digits were swollen and black.

When we arrived late back at the house, she suggested again that I take a bath to warm up. For an hour I lay in her tub under moonlight, listening to her walking around outside, preparing me drinks and popcorn, and leaning against the door every so often to say, "Don't leave! Stay here!" Or, "I love you! Like a daughter . . . or not . . . like, you know, those heroines in the old books, the way they love each other?"

"Celia and Dorothea in *Middlemarch*?"

"Anne Shirley and Diana Barry."

"Jane Eyre and Helen Burns."

But I knew, even then, that our story would only ever be half-written.

The problem with all the white in that house, I would think later, was precisely that it unspooled like the Plains. Pure endlessness, and nothing to contain it. In all the intervening years, I've tried to write that night of the blizzard and the woman I was so desperate to see. But she eludes me. I can remember fragments of what she said, where we went, what we did. We even walked through snow the next morning to visit her old father— an upright man in a wingback chair who eyed me with some confusion; he died two weeks after I left. But the substance of Marianne in my life is unreal and attaches to nothing. That night I seemed to be in a breath of quasi-divine light that—like Dante's light in *Paradiso*—was ready to pierce us with truth. But there was no truth; there was no giving in to form. Marianne was in her own long moment of confronting eternity—the interface of life and death. She was still on a road like the one I had just left: trackless and frightening. She was still wondering where to build her altars and to what. But there was no one to show us the prayer born in the wilderness that was not insubstantial and ghostly, that was a Baby, who gave us a Mother outside of time.

Her phone rang all through the evening and into the night, but she never answered it. Just once, she picked up and held the receiver to her ear before setting it down without saying a word.

I slept in her high white bed, with the cat asleep in a corner on a chair, and she slept down the hallway where she wouldn't disturb me if she coughed. When she came in to say goodnight, she covered the space where her right breast had been with one hand and apologized in advance for keeping me awake. "I can't believe you're going soon. But you're here tonight."

The phone rang sometime in the darkness and I heard a man's voice on the answering machine, a pleading note in what he said. It rang again later, but no message was left. I heard her get up and go into the sitting room, the sound of a spoon in a cup, and long, jagged coughing.

I lay awake at first, wondering why I was leaving, thinking of the Plains' silence that I was still so afraid of. I was too exhausted not to sleep, but something stirred in me deep down as I dreamed. As if I already knew the pain of missing this place, had already heard—how many times—the long American dial tone that never connected.

One face looks out from all his canvases,
One selfsame figure sits or walks or leans:
We found her hidden just behind those screens

"This should be her," I said to myself in a red-walled gallery in Pimlico, London, three years before that white journey through the Plains. I had never seen any picture come so near to Mary.

The painting showed the artist's wife at the moment of death—or *spiritual transfiguration*, the artist said. Her hands are placed palms uppermost as though waiting to receive Communion, her lips are parted, her eyes closed. A haloed dove (the artist's pet name for her was "dove") has descended into her lap like the Holy Spirit, but it is red, the color, also, of passion, and it carries a white flower in its beak, to symbolize the laudanum with which the model killed herself. This model was Elizabeth Siddal, the woman who had lain as Ophelia in a tub of cold water for John Everett Millais. Siddal caught pneumonia from that adventure, and was never strong afterward. As she sickened in the weeks before her suicide, the mind of her husband Dante Gabriel Rossetti was elsewhere. He was entangled with another woman; he was absorbed in his manuscript of poems. When Lizzie died, he placed those poems in her casket in a spasm of guilt, and afterward painted her in this transcendent pose. Here, she is modeling *Beata Beatrix*: Beatrice Portinari, the muse of fourteenth-century poet Dante Alighieri. In the background of the painting stands the grief-stricken Italian poet and an angel who holds in his hand Alighieri's flaming heart (which Alighieri once dreamed that Beatrice ate). I stood there, aged twenty-six, and wished that that painting were of Mary. It would be the end, perhaps, of my quest to find her closest likeness. I saw in it a mystical breaking open, an ecstasy, which was, still, utterly foreign to me, and yet somehow recognizable. What I didn't know, then, was that Elizabeth Siddal, portrayed as Beatrice Portinari, did represent, in a certain sense, Mary. Or if not Mary, one part of her shadows and echoes that would not be expunged from the scourged room of post-Reformation England.

For hundreds of years, English art was dominated, sometimes leadenly, by landscapes and portraits of nobility. Statues and paintings of Mary had been burned. Any public devotion to her had been extinguished. It took a bunch of idealistic Victorian men to begin to look to her, and to God, for their art again. They all, it seemed, tackled the Annunciation, in one way or another: John William Waterhouse's delicate maid in royal blue is stricken in a lilac English spring; Edward Burne-Jones' Mary is pallid as a glass of milk, and his angel's airborne feet are so paradoxically pulled down by gravity that they become the focus of the scene. Dante Gabriel Rossetti painted no less than *three* Annunciations. In one, the angel hovers among the trees, his image reflected in the stream where Mary is bathing her feet. A dove hovers above her head; she looks as though she is being baptized. In another, Mary is reading and seems only vaguely surprised by the angel peering over her shoulder. But it's the first Annunciation that is most famous. Rossetti used his pious, earnest sister Christina as a model for the Virgin. In the painting, Mary, in what looks like a hospital-issue nightie, cowers on her bed like an abused child. She looks anorexic. Behind her is a blue screen of the type seen in hospitals. The angel is in white, like a surgeon. Even back then I sensed that this depiction did not approach the meat and substance of what Christians believed.

No, the only time Rossetti came dangerously close to Mary was when he painted Dante Alighieri's guide to paradise, Beatrice. The girl from Florence with whom Dante fell so hopelessly in love was so idealized by the poet that his passion for her must surely have been a form of transference of his love for the Madonna. As I read the *Commedia* now, how many times do I turn to the notes to find out if love-struck Dante is referring to Beatrice or to the Queen of Heaven?

If the essence of everything I've ever said
of her surpassing beauty was concentrated
within a single note of praise, still it would be
unequal to the wonder I now had before me . . .
beauty that transcends human measure . . .

Mary's beauty is imagined differently by everyone, it seems, but its one immutable characteristic is that it is impossible to describe. "She did not look like that, Monsieur," Bernadette Soubirous told the sculptor when he showed her the official Lourdes statue. "If I had known that morning I would have to go sixty years stuck in this world without seeing her again I don't know how I could have faced it," said a Jewish man who encountered Mary in a dream over one hundred years later. The rightness of the Virgin's beauty is a foretaste of inexpressible rightness. Beatrice, in the *Commedia*, is splashed with that beatitude, bathed in a reflection of God through Mary.

I didn't know any of that in those days in London, the days of Mischa and the irresistible wind. I just looked at Elizabeth Siddal (who, her friends said, looked nothing like the woman in the painting) as Beatrice Portinari (who Dante Alighieri barely knew) as Mary (who Dante, and all of us, were in various ways trying to find), and knew nothing.

I left the gallery that day and stopped at a florist to buy a bunch of Madonna lilies. Those were the days when London's beat and roar were a centripetal force, birthing everything important in the world and in me. My steps were carried with the great peristalsis of workers moving through the streets. The white houses around Regents Park and Kensington shone and towered. I ran up their steps to visit patients, or a lover. Despite the grime, there was so much beauty that it tugged at my sleeve and told me I shouldn't be working. I should be buying up those pink roses and dodecahedrons of white hydrangeas. I should be stepping beyond black railings into squares where plane trees formed a whispering ceiling. I should be hopping off the ambulance at the truck outside the park that sold the best sausage sandwiches in London (and I did). I was charged with the city; I hardly remember being at home. The city carried me off to bed and breathed at me all night outside my window.

So, for the first time, I stopped off at the florist's, and bought the ruinous Madonna lilies. Then I took the tube from Pimlico to High Street Kensington. There was an odd silence in the street that day, and it continued in the train. It fell on everyone: black or white, young or old, suited or in jeans. No one spoke, but eyes locked easily, as though we were all trapped together in some common thought in an underground cave. An old lady in long orange skirts and an African headscarf slumped in a corner, weeping loudly. No one ignored her exactly, but no one asked her if she was okay.

During the short walk to the palace in late August sun, I felt coldly conspicuous: slim, blonde, in long black skirt and top, carrying my lanky, languid blooms: symbols of virginity. There was a general tide going in my direction, and soon I saw the winking ocean of cellophane-wrapped bouquets that I'd seen on the TV news and felt even more awkward about the lilies in my arms. I halted at the shoreline of flowers and, in abject futility and embarrassment, placed my drop of blooms into the plastic sea. "What waste," my nurse manager who was from Zimbabwe would scoff later, "what rank, obscene waste." I stood for a moment at the garlanded foot of the distant palace—which seemed quietly real and nothing to do with anything happening here or on the TV—feeling more distant, not closer, to the woman I supposed I had come to honor.

That Sunday I'd woken early and sloped down, unmade-up and sleepy, to buy bread for breakfast. The Indian-owned shop was remarkably quiet, and the radio was playing lugubrious music on a roll. "We have interrupted our usual programs this morning as a sign of respect for the death"—I assumed the Queen Mother. When a different name was pronounced, I stood still in the dark aisle of the corner shop. By the time I reached the cash register, I was undone in some way I can't recall. Inexplicably in a hurry. I ran back down the road to my flat, noticing on my way an American couple talking, shaking their heads, and nodding to me as if I were local color in an unfurling newsreel.

I was not a royalist. As a twenty-year-old office worker, I had refused the offer to go and stand at the entrance of my workplace to meet her. I was ornery in my republicanism, loosely socialist. But then she became thinner. She began to tell secrets, to say the unsaid. We knew of the bulimia, the sadness, the need to hold and be held. She was unhappy glamour, unhappy brilliance, brutalized femininity—and we loved all that: Elizabeth Siddal, Sylvia Plath, Diana.

In those mystifying weeks, tears rose like a water table from my core and poured down my face with almost no corresponding internal lamentation or thought process. I wasn't alone. On my way into work, the Lebanese man who made my sandwich was red-eyed and broke down when he saw me. Stationery shops, grocers, and cafés had stuck photos of her up in their windows. A homeless man with scabby hands and a grubby eiderdown knelt down on the pavement near the hospital and wept. The receptionist at our clinic had framed an image of Diana that sat on the front desk. Diana was the main topic of staff meetings.

It wasn't the stuff of mass hysteria, we agreed. It wasn't the loquacious depressives who wailed about the death and wanted to kill themselves. It had more the flavor of an unexplained eclipse of the sun, a weird phase of the moon, the distant but catastrophic outbreak of a war. For some, anti-psychotic medication was upped. For others, home visits were brought forward. In those flats, curtains were drawn, meals were unmade. One woman didn't want to get dressed. There was regression and hopelessness. It didn't translate into words; in a sense, it had no name. It was as if an ash cloud covered England. We talked about the death in discussion groups with patients and the rational-dismissive was aired: "It's not like we knew her. It's tragic for her sons, of course, but people are taking it too far." Yet Agatha, a chronic schizophrenic, began hallucinating again, the voices goading her about the meaninglessness of her life. Old Jane, the retired ballet dancer, couldn't come in for therapy—too upset. In psychiatric terms, the death didn't signify one relevant life event that could trigger a breakdown. It was an event in the collective unconscious that acted like a drug on synapses; it swam through neurotransmitters. For that brief period, the element that was Diana was as fundamental in the cultural landscape as an advancing army.

But what was it?

On the portable TV in my nurse's room, she crossed her black-stockinged legs and gazed balefully out of heavily black-rimmed eyes. She wanted to be, she said, "Queen of People's Hearts." She touched people, physically: lepers, AIDS patients, children, anyone. "It's all very well," I said at the time, "to be sympathetic for five minutes, sitting on the edge of a hospital bed in front of the cameras." But I knew the power of touch.

So many of my patients were blind, deaf, incoherent. For them, touch ignited a sense of warmth and calm. It cut through pain and worry. For me, taking a hand provided an index of their distress, their tension, whether they were hot or cold—even their circulation and hydration. You wouldn't buy an orange without handling it. You wouldn't send a pale-faced child to school without feeling their forehead. Touch tells us things. But in England, at the end of the twentieth century, my career was supposed to be focused on nurse-prescribing, management, and targets.

In East Anglia, I returned at weekends to the flat fields and lanes and grey stone churches of my childhood. Always the churches were cold and whitewashed inside. There were no statues, no pictures; the tabernacle was gone, the niches were bare. Only the jewel colors of stained glass remained. Long ago, those churches were like lone ships, and they burned with a cargo of candleflames and images. Touch would have been important— caressing a statue's foot after receiving Communion, the texture of the Host itself on the tongue, the action of striking a match and lighting a candle for the dead. Every single church would have had a statue of the Virgin, crowned in May, taken out in procession in August. People went into churches to warm themselves, to see art that looked like them. They went to see Mary as well as to talk with God. When the Reformers ripped that out, it was like kicking over a hearth-fire and slowly stamping out the embers. Began the long, stolid march of Wesleyan hymns, and no physical contact.

The day of Diana's funeral I was back home, watching with my journalist father, who loved the newsworthiness of the story and the almost treasonous eulogy given by Charles Spencer. The woman whose wedding I had dressed up for at age ten in old net curtains would be laid to rest on an island like the Lady of Shallot. Myth plaited with reality. The groans of the distant crowd were a florid tapestry against which the silent and real devastation of the child princes processed. Story and history, fairytale and personal, bunched and warped. We all cried except my father. He was riveted by the whole thing.

It was just after that he was given three months to live.

One evening, during his last weeks, I staggered upstairs with Dodie, retired West End actress, to see her safely into her flat.

"You're shattered, sister. You should stop for some tea."

We fell onto the couch, and I collapsed against her camel-colored coat. The tears again. Both of us. Me for my dad, her for her husband, dead twenty years, and some regret about a part she didn't take—Lady Macbeth (or was it Nina from *The Seagull*)? And her eyes were packing up. And did I put the milk in the fridge?

"Shh. You're all right, gal. Worse things happen at sea."

She didn't dream of the inappropriateness of any of this. In her dementia, she saw things clearly. "You have a good cry." And we sat there holding hands, looking straight ahead like two people at the cinema.

"Queen of all hearts," Louis de Montfort called the Virgin four hundred years before.

A godlessness swam about me in the days and months following Diana's death as we prepared for my father's death. Dad and I drove out to Bedingham, to a small Saxon church that used to sit alongside another church, Saint Mary's, of which there was now nothing left. The churchyard was ancient, full of leaning stones and sunken graves. In a corner among high nettles and brambles was my grandmother's grave and an aunt's. We walked and looked, especially beyond the low hedge to a field where horses were meandering. It was not a bad spot to be lost. I guessed he must be thinking that soon he would be there, next to his mother, but I was busy with a new camera and thought it would be intrusive to show anything of my guesses. Inside the church, the light was high and clear. And vacant. It was cold.

Like all the other churches thereabouts, there were no statues, no vigilant candle. It was like Good Friday. Again, I took photographs, and saw my father's face assess the nave and pews for a long time. He was grey with thinking. He imagined that his funeral would be there, in a place that felt emptier and more abandoned, almost, than any place I knew. As we drove away, the light was unbearable: stippled with late sun, misty—the invisible imminent made textured and visible.

Why do I return to these days in my mind, just as I return from the prairie? They seem to tell me why I couldn't rest in London. When I came back from my year away in America to recover from my father's death, to recover from Mischa (who had continued to haunt me), I still didn't find what I was looking for. I was no closer to Mary—though I would never have registered that it was her, and her Son, that I sought. Truth be told, I missed the Plains. I was dizzy with longing for the pure space, the evenings with Susan, Jen, and Jenny talking love and liberty. Coming home from readings or poetry workshops or loud bars in London, I would sometimes call Marianne's number and hear that long US ring. She never picked up. But I imagined the sound going through the white house, the cat asleep on the chair in another time of day. I wondered who was listening.

Back in London, I still had the feeling that it was the center of everything, the place where things *happened*. But something was missing. I moved back into the little flat in Mornington Place and took a teaching job. I oozed confidence and tomfoolery. I'd found my voice and wouldn't let myself be subjugated by men again. Going through an old box file of early poems, it's shocking how much I was writing about Mary then—her lap, in one painting, is *the kind to peel apples onto*; her hand is *ghostly on a wall*; her image as Our Lady of Guadalupe is *like a lacquered butterfly*.

I must have bought a little Book of Hours from the British Library around that time. It was a showcase of medieval illuminated manuscripts that depicted the life of the Virgin. In them she was given medieval dress and a pale complexion. She rested in English rose gardens. And the wealthy had themselves added into the scenes. They knelt at her knee. They observed at close quarters her meeting with her cousin or her passing from this world. They crossed that boundary of the literal to put themselves into her life. They needed that touch.

Perhaps it was that touch that I craved.

Marianne takes my hand and tells me not to go. I spend an afternoon looking through the prisms at her window out onto a Midwestern street with its wooden houses and pick-up trucks. In my mind's eye, I pencil myself into her days.

We lose a princess and bury her on an island in the middle of a lake to avoid her grave being overrun by a grieving swarm who have never met her, who think that, somehow, they must be part of her life.

Some years later, I would be telling a little girl not to be scared of the dark. We lived in a modern house five minutes on foot from the hem of the sea and the train track to Rome. At night there was always the hushing roar of water or train; sometimes we couldn't tell which. My little girl was afraid of being alone. She was sweaty with fear at night. I was weary from following her upstairs, and going to soothe her many times a night. "We have to tell ourselves," I explained from a self-help psychology book I'd bought on the subject, "what is real, and what is not real. We should ask ourselves, is it a lion I see? Or just a shadow?"

"What if it's the shadow of a lion?" my seven-year-old answers.

The shadow of a lion is all I could see of the Virgin: thrown signs, ripples on water far from the location of their cause. Her shadows—both inky true and grossly warped by the needs or suggestibility of our minds—were everywhere: in Lucrezia Buti, in pagan goddesses, in dead princesses, in the book of Wisdom, in the Song of Songs.

These glances, these unexplicated, fleeting meetings—Mischa's woman in a hospital corridor, Dante's Beatrice walking along the Arno, Diana dispensing compassion to AIDS patients and leaving in a limousine, even Marianne shambling toward me with a gin and lime—contain the Virgin. In fractured, half-true ways, we mistake people for her. We're like ducklings who've lost their real Mother and imprint onto another.

One year after my return to London, I found myself leaving for a culture that was all about being close to Mary. I packed my suitcase again and put in a postcard of Elizabeth Siddal as Dante's Beatrice.

La Pietà
by Michelangelo, 1498–1499

THREE

Mother

i

Spiritually a "bitter sea" to the demons, officially "star of the sea" to men, eternally "illuminatrix" to the angelic spirits, and universally "lady" to all creatures . . .

I was asleep on an Italian island, and new and unfamiliar stories were happening around me as I slept. Some I would never hear of, some I would read about in newspapers. Some were told by barista to doctor to news agent to the old woman in the laundry until they were written in the town's oral history. Like the strange story of the man across the fields at the base of the mountain, when one night he was woken by the full moon.

At least that's what he thought woke him. The space next to him was empty; his wife had died a year before. He knew it was useless to stay in bed (sleep had become thin), so he rose, poured himself a grappa, and went to say a prayer before a picture of *La Madonna delle Grazie*. He had a lot to thank God for: his land, which was expanding; his sheep, which were growing in number; and his fattening bank account. Then he seemed to remember the sound that woke him—a shuffling outside—and he opened the old front door.

In the moonlight on the path were pale shapes. He could just about see that they were letters spelling out his name. He picked up the letter "F" and felt the shivering of petals and rigid plastic underneath. One by one he brought the wreathes inside and placed them on a table, trying to jumble their order so his name was not written too long.

Too late. He bolted the door, found his hunting rifle, then phoned the police before the fear could grip him.

"What did you do?" the policeman asked when he arrived to find the funeral tributes and the farmer pointing speechlessly at them. But the old man just shrugged.

The flowers were floppy; they shed petals as the policeman eased them into bags. He felt as though he were handling a dead angel, he told his colleagues later—something exotic and improbable. The farmer never blinked all the time he was there. He would not go back to bed that night, nor the nights that followed. The moon kept him company on his vigil, and maybe Mary did too.

But weeks later, once the moon waned, once the blackness crowded out the light, the appointed night came, and at 10 a.m. the next morning, another call came through to the police station. The farmer's body had been found with a bullet through the back of his head. The dots were joined, "justice" done.

It was the sense of time being harnessed to a human narrative that was most disquieting to me about this murder and so many others of which I heard tell. The sense of life's story being overwritten by one damnable, determined human pen. The usual glorious unfolding of things diverted. The violence of an unreasonable edit. I could not get that farmer—who I had never met—out of my head. I pitied him, whatever he had done (or not) to merit his end. But this was the way things were on the island where I had come to live for a time. Justice and retribution were in the hands of the people. It was unlike anywhere I had ever known or would ever know again.

But throughout history and the world, crime is never the exception. Men pitch themselves against wind, steal novices off a street, and, yes, commit murder. They steal sheep—or someone else's wife. From King David to Filippo Lippi to the nocturnal deliverer of floral tributes, the stories never change. We are, all of us, looking to write our own story, sometimes hurrying away from God. Mary is there, though, even and especially in those most dubious of places, her true face hidden in the darkness. She was *La Madonna delle Grazie* on that island. In one mountain town, where she saved the people from plague, she was painted pale and bent to a peach-cheeked son. In a coastal city where she warded off bombs, her statue was dark as an African with cascades of real black hair. Everywhere, she was different. To her ran both the murdered and the murderer.

Even I was flying to her. One March, I found myself hurrying through those ancient streets that were too tight for more than one car, past men in brown velvet trousers and flat caps drinking beer, past dim shops of cigarettes and scratch cards, past gates through which, if you stopped to peer, there were courtyards with ornate and twisted cactus, heavy lemon trees, fig trees, and washing hung from balconies, but no one within. There were half-finished villas of one square story, the roof or upper floor never built, and now, after years, the bare plaster was covered in vines, and the children that had once played in the yard were setting off on scooters that whined through the town, amplifying and fading like gnats. But that day, the streets were empty. Usually there were widows out shopping, all in the same pleated black skirts, shirts, shawls, and headscarves, and the old wives in just the same outfit in brown. There were young mothers in tight jeans and heels so high they tipped the wearer forward as she walked. There were young men in denim jackets, their faces hardened by sun and the morning drink. There were lines of children in blue smocks being shepherded from the church to the park by a nun.

That day, there was no one—till, at the end of the street, in the main piazza, there was a thick crowd pouring down the many steps of the large white church and into the space between bars and the pharmacy with its jars and snakes painted on the windows. There was excitement seething, like the birds in the palm trees. A plastic chair was dragged under a tree for one sparrow-boned widow. A teenager fired a hunting rifle in the air. Then the noon bell tolled, and there was a climactic jostling. On the other side of the piazza, I saw a wooden statue of the risen Christ lifted unsteadily above heads and approaching. The effigy was puppet-like. It bobbed on stiff limbs. Gunshots. Near. I jumped. It seemed impossible that no one would be hit. Then I realized that there was a living body of excitement behind me too. I turned to see another wooden statue—this time of Mary, in a blonde wig and stiff, lacey dress. She looked unlike any image I had ever seen of her: this statue was portly, double chinned, with ringlets and doll-like blue eyes. The kind of woman to inhabit a Victorian drawing room and reprimand servants. The statue was held high and borne to the center, toward the statue of Christ. They approached each other, deadpan and mannered as dancers in a *pavane*. More gunshots, shouts, cheers. Smell of gunpowder.

This scenario was ghoulish and improbable. Even I knew that, in Scripture, the first to see the risen Christ was Mary Magdalene. But, here, it had to be *la mamma* he ran to. *S'Incontru*, they called it—the meeting of the bereaved mother with her resurrected child.

But then, Mary was inflated in that place. I didn't have to search for her in polished galleries and empty spaces. She was at roadside shrines, in bars, in surgeries, in garages and grocers, in schools and police stations. She towered—often above the image of her agonized son. There, Mary's name, it seemed to me, *was* God. Everything was given to *La Madonna*: flowers, rosaries, prayers, exclamations, processions, committees, embroideries, hospitals, prayer cards, blasphemies, promises, babies, songs, and statues—all to her. It actually bored and, in some strange way, appalled me.

"Madonna!" the landlady said when she saw me going out with wet hair. "Madonna!" the cashier gasped when the register jammed. *Madonna, Madonna, Madonna.*

And yet she had never seemed further away. It would be years before I sensed her shadowing me in the dark, not ghostly, as a deer in the darkness, but a woman circling me with her arm.

But then, in that crowd, I was mostly afraid of getting shot. Or crushed. The golden ringlets on the statue wobbled. Birds flew up like shrapnel. Another shot. Children in taffeta or waistcoats were carried on shoulders. Gunshots. Excited chattering and singing in a language I would never learn. *Pro nois prega Maria, quem meruisti portare, / In chelu, in cumpagnia, cherimus tottu cantare.* And then the piazza cleared. People made their way to marinated lamb or pork slow-roasted for days underground. And I wended my way home, alone.

ಬಬ

The old mountain town where my new love was working, and where I found myself that first summer in Sardinia, warped with heat. The streets and houses were carved into a hillside near the sea, though the sea was not visible. Solitary and dark, in summer the streets smelled of myrtle, in spring they pulsed with orange blossom. Yet no matter how hot, there never seemed to be any light. Poverty could be seen in footwear and on faces that looked at outsiders as those who have been locked in windowless cells for years are blinded by a sudden view. The people of the town were uniformly short in stature and unsmiling. Their sons and daughters would grow up to be shepherds, cheesemakers, or shopkeepers unless they took off to the big city or the mainland.

"It's an outpost, a wild island," the new man in my life wrote dramatically on a postcard to me before we were married. Like the people of that island, Fabio was black-eyed and stern. We were hopelessly in love.

"I will marry you," he told me over stuffed vine leaves on our first date in Primrose Hill, some months before I left London. And he wrote on a napkin Catullus' words *Odi et amo*. It didn't occur to me that he was drunk. I had yet to learn that Italians don't drink, at least not in the way that the British do. Within a few months, I had taken him home with me to the country to meet my mother, who, impressed by his sharp suit and impeccable English, asked him to carve the Sunday roast—then watched aghast as he rolled up his sleeves and ripped the bird into sections with his bare hands.

This island man had a way of reflecting, in his deep dark eyes, on all that was said and all that he saw. In the beginning, we rarely argued; there was too much that was different between us; it hardly seemed worth the bother. Instead, we spent weeks exploring England and Italy together, walking the streets of Rome or London, comparing our churches, food, and history. When we pitched up at Temple by the Thames where the crusader knights are buried, I told him I hoped to be laid next to him one day in just such a way: hands grasping a sword, eyes shut, through all of freezing cold eternity. He would quote this back to me twenty years later when I had long forgotten my words.

Eternity. It was a word to empty a London bar. But for an Italian, it was disquietingly normal. In the nick of time, or so it seemed, I was committed to a man who promised to never leave me. Now, at the age of thirty, having shunned so many pictures of Mary with her child, I was seized with the notion that I must reproduce before it was too late, and I was ready to move far from home to do so.

A new picture of Mary had begun to obsess me: Stefan Lochner's fifteenth-century *Madonna of the Rose Bower*, with its multitude of roses, and angels with small heads supporting and surrounding her like a luscious, loose-weave fabric. Lochner's Mary looked, ironically, like that other Virgin Queen, Elizabeth I: anemically white, lashless, with ginger hair and scarce eyebrows. Only her belly swelled beneath the heavy blue dress—for the rest, she was frail as a twelve-year-old after the flu. But her crown was gem-laden and colorful as a sweetshop, the baby was good, and the little strumming angels looked eager to help. I told bemused friends I would hang a print of it in the nursery.

That first summer on the island, I was often left alone in the evening while Fabio worked. Undaunted, I would set off through the dark streets in search of someone who could open a door to me and make the place come real. Mary met me, as painting or ceramic statue, at every corner, but there she seemed as foreign as everyone else. I wandered in and out of leather and ceramic shops and learned that browsing was not a thing that was tolerated. Sometime in my first week, I decided to ignore the invisible barrier that kept me from going into a bar in the piazza. Outside on plastic chairs, shepherds in flat caps were drinking beer or grappa. It didn't matter what time of day: from 10 a.m., there was always a group of them outside the bar. I walked through the heavy odor of sheep cheese and stepped into a dark cavern of smoke, lit, it seemed, only by beer and the lights of eyes. Wolfish was how the younger men seemed. And the older stared me down. No one smiled. I ordered a *Vecchia Romagna* (my new tipple) and drank it quickly on my feet. As I turned to leave, I saw, in a corner, a young blondish woman sitting on the knee of a young shepherd. She grinned at me. I knew, just by the fact of that smile, that she wasn't from the island. "Hello!" I called lightly through the smoke. But she just gave a wave and turned back to her lover.

I never returned to the bar. I was having to sniff out different danger signs—signs from fifty years ago or more. Signs that belonged nowhere else but here, in this ancient town, where

"DDT" in large painted letters could still be read on front doors and people wedged euros and promises under the ceramic foot of the Madonna. Soon after that brief drink, a man would be gunned down in the street in broad daylight. After that, another man was shot at point-blank range in a bar. What struck me most was the abject acceptance of these shootings by the people of the town as they stolidly cleaned up the blood and carried on.

"Of course," Giorgio, the barista at the new café, told me with a shrug. "They had it coming."

"Christ stopped at Eboli," my GP explained on my first visit to her with nervous indigestion, "and he also stopped here"—meaning *stopped short of*, not *stopped for a visit*, as the bad translation sounds. "*Stai attenta*. Be careful."

Susan of the Plains did stop by, though, on her way to Rome to stay with a lover she had met online. She rambled the streets of the twisted town as though they were the prairie, her taupe hair covering half her face and an unlit roll-up in her hand. Once we had hugged hard and long, she immediately unrolled her yoga mat on our *terrazzo*, and each morning we greeted the sun over the hills together. She sketched the twisted cactus in our yard and said she would sculpt it when she got back home. We reminisced about my college days and the nights with Jen and Jenny (who had split up by then; Susan was looking for new lodgings). But we lacked that particular blend of leisure, purpose, and ease that we'd always had on Magnolia Street. Here, on austere marble-tiled floors, Susan put her hair up and let me see her lips twitch with the need for a story.

One night, when Fabio and I had retired to bed at 10 p.m., Susan let herself out of the apartment and went drinking in the forbidden bars, with the fugitives, soused shepherds, and drug dealers. She had a fine time, she told me later, listening to local song, downing grappa, climbing in the back of a truck for a trip up the mountain to an old monastery whose doors were shut and locked under the stars. She returned to us at 3:30 a.m., tiptoeing across the tiles and filling the hallways with the stench of cigarettes. Fabio was incandescent with rage. She could have been killed, she must have been raped, she had compromised us; we couldn't be associated with those kinds of people; she was a child; why couldn't she grow up? This wasn't America. Next morning, I found Susan sitting on her bed with her bag already packed. Whether she heard what Fabio hissed at me in the dead of night, I never knew. She carefully and tearfully counted out her euros for her onward journey and promised me that she did think my fiancé "worthy of me." Her eyes were as strained and hopeful as they had been that day we conducted the spell to the goddess in the snow.

There was something terrible about Susan's departure, a tableau that disclosed some fundamental change in my life for the years to come. From my balcony, I watched her walk in her short cotton dress down the dusty mountain road to the bus stop. As she stepped on the bus, she seemed to take freedom with her. I was left with the heavy mantle of living in a Mediterranean society where you had to choose: you either set the fires or watched them from a distance. Or were burnt.

๛

In October, we took off further south to where, my new love assured me, life was friendlier. The journey by car was miles of nauseous mountain bends, broken by pitstops in boar-infested woods. "Nearly there, nearly there," he kept saying, until we finally reached a dark house at the end of a very long dark lane at the bottom of a mountain. Fabio's parents had no idea that they were expecting a guest. Their villa loomed long-eyed behind them as they tottered out to greet the car. They led us into a room that was bare and dimly lit, furnished with beach recliners for armchairs, a long table with two benches, and nothing else. As we set down our bags, they swore at Fabio in Sardinian, trilled at us both in Italian, and hurriedly put together bread, sheep's cheese, grapes, and a carafe of red wine. They had never been outside Italy. They couldn't understand how this messy-haired girl from England had blown into this corner of the world with their son. Where were my parents?

Next morning, I woke alone to see a sunny olive grove, fields, and the deep blue sea through my window. When I crept down for coffee, my future husband was talking fast and pacing the road out front with his earnest-looking father. But his mother seemed quite gleeful to see me as she sculpted pieces of pasta in the kitchen and pressed another homemade donut on me. We passed those first few days in the blessing of mutual incomprehension.

It was only when I took it into my head to do certain things that the parents became restive. If I wanted to go for a walk alone, or go to the bar to recharge my phone, I was blocked with shrieks and waving arms. Walking alone was inadvisable, my husband croaked from his siesta slumber: sheepdogs would attack me, and the bar was full of shepherds; it wasn't safe. I took to pacing the olive grove while they all slept. But sometimes I stole the car keys and drove down to the beach to walk by myself, determined to somehow make all of this silence and beauty my own.

In those early days, and even years, the Italian language was a veil that muffled everything. After meals, as Fabio's mother or father talked to me, my eyes would ache and burn—as though I was literally straining to see what it was they were saying. And they wanted to tell me everything; they wanted to give me their version of events, to recount the defining moments of their lives, give the prosecution and defense accounts of their marriage. I somehow learned that the cheese I ate was produced from a flock that pastured on the family land. That the ten-minute drive to

the nearest town was done by horse and cart when his mother
was a child. That the electric lights were new, and generally dis-
trusted as magnets for mosquitoes.

"Look!" my father-in-law widened his black eyes at the end
of lunch, and showed me his empty plate. "I don't eat apples in
May. Why?" He waited for many seconds, as if I might really
know the answer. "As a promise to *La Madonna*. Why?" He widened his eyes farther still and leaned back his bald head with the
force of what he had to impart, one finger raised. "Because one
day, when I was ten, the Virgin saved my life. It was in the little
town where we all lived: me, my mother and father, my two sisters, and brother. My father was just back from the war and food
was still short. The American soldiers would hand out sweets
and sometimes even eggs, but we were hungry. Every day we
were hungry. One day in May, my school friends and I decided
to steal apples from a garden by the church. The trees were full
of fruit! We climbed the church wall to reach the branches and
began to fill meal sacks with apples. I climbed the highest—I
was smallest and it was easiest for me. Then, the bough I was
balancing on snapped, and I went tumbling down into the garden. It was a long way! A very long way. I could have been killed
quite easily. But I landed on a haybale, completely unharmed. Of
course, then I had to reclimb the tree and find my way back over
the church wall before I was seen. It was the Madonna who saved
me! She gave me the soft landing! I promised her I would never
eat another apple in the month of May, her month. And I've kept
my promise for seventy years."

It wasn't just the parents who wanted to talk to me. The clus-
ter of houses by the sea were all populated by relatives. An uncle
lived on one side and an aunt on the other. Another aunt lived
across the field, and an uncle down the road, another in town, and
yet more uncles, aunts, and cousins were in every shop and bar.
Here, I could counter the baleful gaze of butchers and baristas

by saying I was part of their clan. It unlocked any situation (even with my blonde hair and height). It got me the best prosciutto, a good price, a seat in a restaurant, and common courtesy. But no encounter was casual. When the patriarch died, leaving no will to speak of aside from a scribbled note saying which riding breeches he wanted to be buried in, a decades-long wrangle began over fields, houses, apartments, and pathways. It wasn't just this family: every islander was part of a dynasty and, therefore, of a feud, whether over a water supply, boundary, or property. If I ignored someone in the street accidentally, a conciliatory phone call or drink had to be urgently arranged. If I greeted someone in the grocer's that I was not meant to be friendly toward, there was an evening of shouting and swearing, dinner left cold, and the fire unlit as people stomped off to bed. Going for a coffee in the morning was exhausting, as Fabio methodically worked the bar, shaking hands, assessing, buying coffees, accepting pastries, like a delegate at the United Nations in a world forever on the brink of war.

It was hard to know if the family's epic rows, gothic threats, and tendencies to brandish kitchen utensils were simply cultural or a sign of something darker. When my mother-in-law brought in a pigeon that the cat had killed to roast for our lunch, Fabio thrust the mophandle to the ceiling as though it were a sword and yelled so loudly that the aunt across the field came running. But with me, he was puppy-eyed and malleable. He had always been misunderstood, he said. I understood him; I was his *Madonnina.*

Sometime in those early days, my future mother-in-law took me up a mountain miles from the sea to visit one of her elderly friends. The woman's son had killed himself a year before, Fabio's mother briefed me as we careered around the country lanes, and we needed to enliven her, encourage her to get out of the house, make her see that grief, ultimately, had to be left behind. I don't know how I understood what Fabio's mother told me, but I usually did: she, like many islanders, spoke perfect Italian, like the school-taught language that it was to them.

"Don't mention her son!" she finished up as we began to ascend the mountainside. "Just talk about lunch and going to the sea. She needs to go to the sea." The sea was the cure for everything.

Signora Angelica's house was hemmed in on all sides by almost vertical vineyards and sheer red rock. On the last stretch of road to reach her front door, the climb was so steep that the car barely moved forward in first gear, and my mother-in-law barked for me to get out before we rolled backward down the hill.

Once we'd abandoned the car at an angle across a track, the help lady Ngozi opened the door and led us into a room that was almost empty aside from a long polished table covered in doilies. The back wall of this room was dominated by a canvas, about eight feet by six, which showed a grey house on a rock in a furious sea. In the midst of the raging waves, there was a tiny boat that leapt with its own lightness and seemed about to crash against the house. The house was empty. Its windows were the shape of eye sockets.

I knew that the dead son was an artist, and I guessed that it was he who had painted this. The rest of the room was as ascetic as any other *salotto* on the island: church calendar on a wall, a bottle of pills on a table, painted ceramics holding apricots. You rarely saw a book, a magazine, or a game left out in an island home. If there was a picture on the wall, it was of the sea—a representation of exactly what could be seen out of the window. Pictures of Mary were common but were kept for the bedroom unless, as Fabio put it, its owners were religious maniacs.

No one had a picture like this on their wall. It roared behind the bent old lady. The sea, the house, and the helpless boat were embodiments of torment. They were trapped in a world of raging

pain. Further up the hillside, its creator, left by his wife and as-
phyxiated by heartbreak, had hanged himself one lonely night.

My mother-in-law rattled on to Signora Angelica about the
state of the water and the necessity of getting out. She complained
at length about her stiff neck and blamed the wind direction and
the damp. (In Italy and its islands, the four winds carry all kinds
of psychological and physical states.) As she chattered on, Signora
Angelica was a lifeless heap. Her lace-trimmed handkerchief was
transparent with tears, and she kept pressing her face into her
hands like someone in bodily pain. My mother-in-law talked
on cheerily about the new priest, the pasta we were having for
dinner, Signore Arturo's psoriasis. She was worried about a procession she was organizing for the sorority of Santa Rita and also
a cousin who'd become involved with a cheesemaker who was
young and handsome but had just come out of prison. Signora
Angelica wasn't interested. She pushed a dish of sugared almonds
toward me and looked out the window.

"What an impressive painting," I leaned forward to her,
speaking in faulty Italian. "Your son?"

My mother-in-law gave a sharp little gasp and turned away
with theatrical embarrassment. Signora Angelica looked doubt-
ful but turned to me and nodded. Then started to talk. And talk.
I couldn't understand what it was she said, but she started to
cry, and Fabio's mother leapt to her feet and hissed that this was
my fault.

"Look!" I kept saying, fumbling for some of my very few
words and pointing at the painting. "Look! How beautiful."
Meaning, he is here in the room with us; I can't ignore him.
He won't be ignored. His abandonment, his affliction are thundering through us as we sit among the doilies and the ceramic
bowls. His Calvary casts shadows.

This artist, I would learn later from stories told in the town,
married a woman when he was twenty-two and she just eighteen.

He thought there was a specialness in her, an innocence. She was training to be a hairdresser and was full of dreams about moving to the mainland and having her own salon near Rome. She was too beautiful for the island, or so she believed. The island's women all learned how to make shell-shaped pasta stuffed with potato and sheep's cheese. They all knew how to dance the traditional shuffle of their land. They knew how to dress their hair, and skin rabbit and lamb. But she had dreams beyond all of that. The sheep and lambs could be butchered by other people. She was dreaming Neapolitan pizza, shish kebabs, bagels, and burgers. Still, for two or three years, she looked up to the artist and followed him everywhere. He seemed to have the key to the greater, wider world, with his paintings and his nights out drinking in the clubs in the city. But then, four years after the wedding, she was gone.

He'd tried to dismiss some special intonation or carelessness when she said a name. He'd tried to shake off the doubt he had when he saw a condom wrapper in her handbag one night. The shattered clues were too disparate. He kept reassuring himself it was his own paranoia. Until he was told she had left town in a trailer with a man from Naples.

Some truths are too large and ugly to see or swallow. They are whale-like, rank. The fact of his wife's desertion loomed over him and blocked his path. It was as if he had to eat his way through it. Not simply know it, but actually take it in his stomach and let it become part of himself. He could not do it. He could only think:

Stop.

There is often a lit window at some distance from these dark nights—perhaps at a great physical distance—where a mother shadows the pain. (I think, these days, of the Garden of Gethsemane and where Mary might have been as she waited through Jesus' agony.) Signora Angelica was doubtless tethered to her son's misery. But she can't have known how he would find a rope and teach himself (expertly, quickly) how to fashion a noose. How he would search the house for a place to hang himself up like a coat, and test a hook on the wall. How he kicked the chair away. How it dawned on him, as his feet scrabbled and his eyes bulged, that life is a larger fact than the whale-like obstacle that stood in its path. It is not so easily destroyed.

But he did destroy it. With the violence of his own unreasonable edit, he died. This is all his story.

But his mother is the subtext, the backstory, the new angle, the director's cut; the voice that takes up the scream of an anguished life when it has run so long and so deep that it thinks it can sustain no longer.

The artist's final word stayed with us in the form of his painting. It was his howl, caught like a bat's webby wings in sticky paint. One day, it will degrade, become lost, end up in someone's cellar or in a flea market where a student will buy it and leave it propped behind a door. But his mother's pain will never be lost. There will be no forgetting. It will sweep through her form and mark her, heartbeat by heartbeat forever, as years mark the trunk of a tree.

More than a decade after meeting Signora Angelica, I would be sitting in a walled garden in the center of Rome. There was peace, and green parrots were eating cumquats from a tree. An elderly friar in a long white habit was talking and laughing. We were discussing motherhood, and he told me about one of the visions experienced by St. Teresa of Avila. Teresa was a strong, determined woman, but was given, like so many poets, to episodes of despair. Once, when she was feeling low, she had a vision that Christ came to console her. He told her about a time that he had consoled his mother. Mary was indeed the first person that he met after his Resurrection. And she was so agonized by what she had witnessed that she could not rejoice immediately at the sight of him. He had to stay with her a long time because her soul was so *transpierced*. He had to soothe her for her to come back to herself and realize the Joy that stood before her.

His mother treasured all these things in her heart

At Signora Angelica's, the Nigerian help lady brought us *limon-cello* and almonds baked in sugar and lemon juice. We talked about the cousins, who is buying a car, who failed their school year. Signora Angelica would be conveyed mercifully through the mountainous regions of grief—the denial, the anger, the bargaining, the depression, the acceptance—but, like Mary in Teresa's vision, her son's agony would stay with her, like a stone she had swallowed. She would learn to walk with its weight—that's all. She would begin to bake her *ciambellone*, to laugh, to walk barefoot in the shallows beyond the mountains. But nothing would erode that stone.

Signora Angelica turned to me that afternoon. She was, wetly, delighted to talk about her son, and it made her smile at me as she hadn't done before. My mother-in-law pulled me out of my chair and, complimenting her friend's geraniums loudly, then said we had to go home.

Her smile evaporated as we left the apartment.

"What did you have to go and say that for?" she said as we walked down the steps to the car and lurched back down the hill.

My prickly relationship with my mother-in-law was a sign of my failure to adapt to life in this new place. Like the island it-self, she tried to hobble my unconventional ways and to paralyze my tongue with food. If I would only eat the kilo of pasta she cooked and drink the grappa, I would sink into a beach recliner and not wander out or speak up. The dinner table became a battle-ground on which I refused everything but the smallest plate of pasta and a plum. She repeated like a mantra "Mangia, mangia,

mangia!" ("Eat! Eat! Eat!") through those three-hour banquets, which only made me eat less. I thought that the eating disorders units on the island must be bursting.

The coffee and wine she gave me before our journey back to the dark town were ruinous. By the time we arrived, it hurt very much to use the bathroom. That night, Fabio worked late, and I walked to the pharmacy to find something herbal for cystitis but mistranslated the packet and bought a diuretic instead. Bewildered, I began passing blood and had to rustle up the on-call doctor, who wearily brought me a prescription for antibiotics. "*Stai attenta!*" ("Be careful!"), she said again. I was beginning to feel like I was allergic to the island.

ii

O you who dwell in the gardens,
my companions are listening for your voice

The summer after our wedding was the hottest anyone could recall. When we drove down the mountain to the sea, even the seawater was the temperature of tears. Even the cicadas fell silent; the mosquitoes died. Life took a siesta until well after sundown when people congregated in the piazza to drink beer or *limoncello*. Fabio was working long hours. He couldn't get a day off, not even a Sunday.

Every morning she rang me:
"Still hot?"
"I don't know. I'm wondering if it's lifted a little . . ."
"It looks misty over the marshes."
"The radio says there are three more dead from the heat."
"Shall we risk a coffee? Lunch?"
"I'm sweating and it's eight in the morning."
"See you after dark then?"
"Absolutely."

She was the blonde on the shepherd's knee I saw in the bar that afternoon of the *Vecchia Romagna*. Liz, as she was called, was my age, and Scottish. She'd lived in the town for a couple of years but, unlike me, had found her niche. She loved life in those dark streets and their proximity to the sea. She loved that there was nothing to do but go to bed in the afternoons and nothing to wear but sundresses. She was utterly sun-kissed, from her brittle blonde hair to her tender rose-gold tan. Like me, she spoke so fast she slurred her words and laughed so easily that everything was a joke. Slouching through evening heat to her basement apartment made me taste, just slightly, the old freedoms.

But, unlike me, Liz had other friends. Soon I was drinking regularly with them and their dark-eyed circle, discussing poetry in the most basic terms, and learning how the Spanish colonized their culture and the Piedmontese cut down their forests and ran off with the wood. It happened hundreds of years ago, but they'd never gotten over it.

"Her husband's very handsome," Liz told them one evening, as she took a lasagna out of the oven and lit a cigarette. "Show us a picture," commanded one of the young men. I took out my wallet and proudly showed them a photo of Fabio. All the group sat up and carefully studied it, passing it around, looking at one another. One of the women flicked her ash across the table, catching the eye of a man too far away to nudge. He looked up and she winked at him, miserably.

"Who is this 'Liz'?" my husband kept asking when he came home from work. We would often drive out of town and down to the beach in the evenings. A fisherman told him that when the temperatures were this high, the only place to get cool was at the very edge of the sea. Not even the beach—right where your feet got wet. So we stood on that border and felt the almost-fresh air on our skin. Fabio couldn't square the fact of a woman like Liz living alone in a strange town. He was also very suspicious of Liz's circle. The island operated under a particular form of apartheid: the Respectable and the Unrespectable. The Respectable did everything they could to maintain what Italians call *la bella figura*. For this group, at the most basic level, floors had to be washed daily, shoes had to match handbags, school marks had to be high. The hostess tray had to be filled with the right kind of cakes and the right cut of meat had to be served with the right herbs. The Unrespectable challenged or ignored these—and a thousand other—subtle rules. They went out at the wrong hours. They read the wrong books and smoked weed. At night they drank and got high, as Susan-from-the-Prairie had done. I would hear them roaring down the empty streets at 2 a.m. or shouting to each other outside bars. These people were cash-in-hand; they built houses illegally. They drove without licenses and rode horses and Vespas without helmets.

But sunny Scottish Liz, to me, was normal. Our language bound us, and we laughed at the same things. I only made those silent streets my own when I sat on our villa steps one night with Liz, drinking white wine and singing at the starry sky. Yet Liz talked the island talk far better than I ever would: she possessed an island persona that was intelligent and sexy. She worked as a lifeguard in summer and a cashier in winter. She cooked *carbonara* and listened to Italian news all the time. She horsed around in the piazza at night and threw gravel at my window to wake me, as Fabio dragged me back to bed. And then, one day, shortly after the night I dined with her friends, she disappeared.

I made the usual morning phone call, but it went repeatedly to the answering machine. On the third day of no word, I braved the hallucinatory heat to reach her apartment. It was shuttered. Her neighbor, an old lady with five cats, was out watering her rosemary and shrugged unhelpfully when I asked if she'd seen Liz. "Inghilterra?" ("England?"), she threw out as I walked away. As I mooched back across town, I reasoned that Liz must be staying with friends or must have taken a trip to one of the smaller islands. But it was odd that she hadn't told me.

After days of hearing nothing from her, I tried to resume my old routines. The lanky barista in the bar on the corner told me he had seen Liz one morning, so I knew that she was alive at least. I was left with the indigestible fact that she wasn't answering my messages.

One afternoon, Fabio came home from work and told me we were going for a drive. We headed down the long road to the sea and then walked along to a forest that bordered the beach. In the shade of pine trees, we sat and stared at the sand dunes.

"I'm really sorry." He was looking straight ahead. "I've already phoned your mother."

This didn't surprise me, whatever was coming next. The figure of the mother in Italy is always more important than anyone else. My mother had been absent from my decision-making for more than a decade. I could imagine her coming in from her English garden to answer Fabio's phone call, watering can in hand, and wryly listening to a logic to which she would always be a stranger.

"You won't be seeing Liz anymore," he declared. "I know what's happened: she's been warned off you, and I'm here to warn you off her. You're a member of my family now. If you're with that kind of person, it doesn't just taint you. It taints me, my family, my work. People doubt our word, our money."

"Why? How would that even happen? I'm not doing anything wrong."

It didn't matter how he tried to explain. I knew that he couldn't explain. The consequences of who you were seen with, who you ate with, or who bought you a drink seeped into your life and affected everything. The island's social structures operated on a butterfly effect system that even Fabio didn't really understand. He just knew who to avoid, what to embrace, and—like so many islanders that I knew—-to keep his distance from everyone.

I didn't argue. It seemed pointless to say that, where I was from, Liz did nothing wrong. The definition of sin had changed with the landscape and my marriage. I was a signora now. I had to have a new, more suitable coat, my mother-in-law informed me, and jewelry. It was the end of the season. The beach was deserted, though the water was still very blue and warm.

"But there's something else," Fabio was saying. "You can't say this to her. You can't speak with her. You ignore her now. No phone calls. Never say any of this to her. Never mention my name."

"I'll write to her."

"No! Worse! Nothing. Nothing at all. She's out of our life."

It is a measure of the fragmentation of my sense of self—and my fearfulness of the shootings and fires that punctuated island life—that I did not disobey him. For the first time in my life, I was conscious of wanting to be safe.

In the following weeks, the town became dead to me again. I made my daily journey to the supermarket to try and fail to get the meat I wanted. I washed the floors (a new skill), and once the sun had lowered, I climbed the hill to *La Madonna della Solitudine*, where the remains of a famous island writer, Grazia Deledda, were kept. The church was simple, almost empty. I remember no notable statue of Mary. There, I remembered how Liz had wanted to paint a picture for the cover of my first poetry book of a red dress flapping on a pole on the beach. In the church, I did not speak about Liz to God; I still did not believe in him. I certainly did not speak to Mary. I only felt the solitude physically squeeze my heart.

It was a new kind of aloneness. Not the loneliness of watching Susan walk away down the mountainside nor the isolation of seeing Mischa's partner walk down the street. Fabio and I were trying and failing to have a baby, and it was the vacancy of my own body that crowded my mind. It turned out that the pregnancy I had scrupulously avoided with pills and rubber for so many years wasn't so easy to get. I thought my body would respond to biological freedom like a log embracing gravity as it falls off a wall. Instead, it dumbly refused to comply. We did not, on the surface of it, let this get us down. On the days of disappointment, we always went out for dinner, or sometimes into the center of the island to stay in a *pensione* and glut ourselves on homemade *sebadas* (deep-fried pastry filled with pecorino and lemon, smothered in honey). Once, we drove to another smaller island where we watched flamingoes arabesquing on the evening sands. But every beauteous, satisfying thing seemed pointless if I could not fulfill this desire that I had always scorned: to be a mother.

And then, the day the rain came down, Liz called me. It was coming to the end of summer, and the most monstrous storm exploded from the sky; drops the size of marbles fell and were as warm and soft as blossom on the skin. As they doused the scorching dust outside, I ran down onto the track and stood with my face up to the heavens. Somehow Liz's call seemed provoked by the same barometric shift. How had I listened to my husband? Liz and I were friends and British. He could never understand what kind of person she was. Nor what bound us.

The sun turned its hot breath away and ribbons of cool ran through the town. I stopped at a perfume shop to buy soap decorated with dried flowers for Liz and then to a bar to collect chocolate *cornetti* for our breakfast. As I arrived at the little courtyard of Liz's basement flat, I was hit by the smell of old cigarettes.

Inside, she was making coffee. Though her face was blotchy with crying, she threw her arms around me when she saw me, and laughed.

"I'm sick."

I stepped back.

"No. Don't worry. Get some plates and sit down."

We waited almost in silence for the coffee to brew. I arranged pastries on a large plate and took it to the table outside. I could smell flowers again after the rain, and wet stone. I could breathe more easily and think better in the cool. When she joined me on the plastic seat, she took my hands.

"I'm pregnant."

I had a strange sense, at first, that she had spoken my line. I felt—almost—like a woman who is robbed as she stands innocently in the street. I watched her expression forensically, wondering if she had this wrong. No, I thought, *I* have it wrong. It must be me who is a mother. Surely? These thoughts were less than a second. They gave way to my own heavy disappointment. Then, a creeping wariness—as if I guessed the only way that this could go.

The silence hovered. Our heads were bent together—like the angel and Mary in room fifty-eight of the National Gallery, I would think later. But I didn't want those wings. I didn't want to be the fleshless spectator. Nothing and no one breathed. She looked so closely into my eyes that I could see the flecks of yellow against the brown of her irises.

"What do you think about that?" I was the first to speak.

"I don't know."

I swallowed and took a wild chance. "Well, I think it's wonderful."

"You do?"

"Yes!"

"I'm not with the father. Not anymore. I haven't got any money."

"It's ok. You'll have help. It will be ok. Maybe you'll go home?"

"No. I think this is a great place to bring up a child. Don't you?"

"I do."

No one mentioned abortion. I had the feeling that this was a narrative that Liz's life needed. A child had dropped into her lap. Suddenly, this being dictated everything about her empty hands and arms, everything she would do. We went out shopping, I

remember, and bought baby magazines and yellow-knitted bootees from the old *cartoleria* by the pharmacy. We talked baby
names and hospitals, and I wondered if I would conceive soon
too, and we would go through this thing together. As we sat
down on the steps of the big church with ice cream, I noticed
a shepherd leaning drunkenly against a wall outside the bar,
watching us.

Shortly after that day of news, I had Liz over for lunch. Fabio knew of my little break in routine but didn't comment. I was
invited to Liz's for the evening in turn, but when I arrived with
a bottle of red wine, there were no other guests at the carefully
laid table. Each one had canceled at the last minute. "When they
knew I was coming," I wanted to say to Liz, and perhaps did say.
She would have denied it. Her smile was determined, and we
lazily ate the olives and lasagna, and I drank the wine anyway.
Another evening, I saw her with her group of friends in the piazza and our eyes met, but Fabio pulled me around abruptly to
greet our old landlord who was out for the *passeggiata* with his
wife. When I tried to turn back to Liz, he told me again that it
was over. "Look who she is with!"

Yes, I knew who she was with. They were the shepherds in
the all-day bars, the ones that Susan had disappeared with that
night before her departure. I didn't call Liz. I even ignored her
calls. I had Fabio's family at my back, watching, guiding, sug-
gesting I go down south to "rest."

Then, one morning, I took a phone call from an English
woman I had once met who lived in the next town. Enid had
been on the island for a full forty years and was more island
now than English. She lived next door to the village church and
did all the flowers and cleaning and organized every event. She
knew all the expats, too, and helped us out with the labyrinthine
bureaucracy.

"Have you heard from Liz, *cara*?"

I said that I hadn't.

"*Madonna*. It's just that she was going out West for an abortion, and I wondered if she'd asked you to go with her."

I said no and hung up, not caring if I seemed rude, just looking out at the awful heat as if there was something to see.

It was not long after that that I heard Liz had left the island, though where she went I don't know. I felt no moral indignation at her choice, just an insidious guilt at ignoring her calls. Fabio and I headed down south again. His parents had taken the boat to Rome to stay in their house on the other side of the sea and sort out mail and money issues. We had quiet days together, Fabio painting bedrooms and me helping out, but falling into laden silences. I couldn't digest this edit of Liz's story. I felt foolish for buying the knitted yellow bootees. Foolish about everything. A *scirocco* wind pummeled us all day and night. It was a wind unlike any I had ever known: it riffled the house. Pictures slid off walls and small tables overturned. Everything was coated in the red dust of the Sahara. I couldn't read or write. I dreamed ringing phones and doorbells and being unable to get through doors that had no handle. Many times I dialed Liz's number but never made the call. Regret was so close and large within me that I would never fathom its real shape or size.

I became even more desperate to leave the island and to begin a family. Both seemed unobtainable. At the end of summer, we joined Fabio's family for the *festa* of Santa Sofia. Every year, the statue of the saint was carried from the main church in town through narrow streets and up a steep mountainside, where Mass was celebrated outside a tiny chapel. Three days later, the statue was processed back down the mountain, the crowd following, praying the Rosary in their language. Gunshots were fired as usual, horses reared and were ridden pell-mell down the streets; riders were thrown. Every year it was the same. We climbed up on the Friday in uncomfortable heat. By the descent on the

Sunday evening, autumn had come; we often stopped at a market stall when we reached town to buy a sweater or a shawl.

Every year the discussion was the same: Who would climb, and if not why not? My father-in-law's heart wasn't strong enough. Could *la bambina* manage it? Would it rain? Was it too hot? Should we drive up? (The road was winding; only the very frail were driven.) But up we went. Even those who didn't go to Mass through the year went. And those who didn't go gave me money—five or ten euro—to place at the feet of the statue. One aunt, whose son was very ill, gave me money and asked me to pray. And every year we climbed—families and gangs of elderly, teenagers, and children. And every year, I told anyone who would listen that they had the wrong statue. The effigy borne high ahead of us was tall, dressed in green, and had *a crown of twelve stars*. Like the woman in the book of Revelation, I spluttered—so she's Mary, not Sofia. No one cared. They couldn't wait to give her their money, then get down the mountain to fairground rides and pizza. Not only did they treat Mary like a goddess; they confounded her with Santa Sofia. The notes and coins that they gave to the statue were something like the birds that the Virgin took to the temple as a sacrifice long ago.

I was still not asking Mary for anything. When a baby still did not arrive, we made an appointment with a specialist, who asked me about my cycle and scanned me, then sighed and rubbed his eyes. "Signora, it takes time. Patience!" It had been more than a year. The last Easter Sunday, I went alone again to *S'Incontru*. It was the same as ever. The old widow in black was seated under a palm tree, the children were decked out in taffeta and waistcoats, the gunfire was still more. How shabby and feeble the wooden statue of Christ looked. How strange the Virgin was: just a blue-eyed doll. But the flowers were extravagantly scented, and the excitement rose in one breath and voice. It was Mary Magdalene who first witnessed the resurrected Christ, I wanted to shout. They wouldn't have cared. Here, they seemed to know what Teresa of Avila knew: that God had to visit the Virgin first. And they seemed to think that *this* event—the meeting between the risen Jesus and Mary—eclipsed all other, broader considerations of the Resurrection, such as the salvation of the world, the fulfillment of God's promises, or the beginning of Christianity as the world knows it. I could feel this pulsing thread that the people had pulled out of that elaborate and vast tapestry, and how it beat through them. I saw the blank faces of parents who had lost their teenager in a car accident one night. (There were many teenagers lost in car wrecks on that island.) I saw Liz's face in my head, the confused, unflickering colors of her irises. And Signora Angelica's transparent handkerchief. I imagined, too, the stupefied face of the man who received his own funeral wreaths. And the faces of anybody who had lost anybody. Anyone who knew a bad ending. This was their story, the part of salvation they particularly wanted and needed: the mother's divinely inspired bond with her son, salvaged, unbroken, out-of-time. The Virgin's sorrow—her son's terrible murder—taken, and her outlandish, almost beyond-human love given succor. Christ was theirs. But, just as much they felt, so was she. He was the giver; she, like them, was the receiver. The prime witness that the broken could be healed.

And this, now, I began to see is what Mary is: conduit of divinity to humanity, more woman than any. She holds the pain that mothers hold and cannot lose because they keep it all: the baby teeth, the locks of hair, the drawings and notes. They are depositories of dreams and trauma, disappointments and pain. She grieves with all of us in our eternal grief. She grieves even if we forget how to grieve. She grieves for Christ in his agony when we become nonchalant or forgetful. She prays for us all to be like her, vividly alive in our love and our sorrow for her son— whether we are the conquered or the conqueror, the good or the bad, the murdered or the murderer. Because, in that final *pietà* as she holds her son's body, she is the Mother of Mercy who holds Everything. And she holds us with him so we can enter his heart.

The days shortened, the damp returned, Christmas came and went. I was still not pregnant. Fabio had secured a job on the mainland in Rome. As I packed up our belongings to leave the island forever, I came upon a package that Liz had given me just after we first met. I had wanted to like the gift so much, but I quite literally couldn't abide it, so had shoved it in the back of a cupboard where I couldn't see it. On the pink tissue paper was written "For Sally," and inside was a framed picture of the Virgin. It was a contemporary portrayal of the Madonna that I squinted at anew. She was cloaked crown to foot in a white sheet like a burqa: she had no face, no feature, no detail. She was a ghostly goddess, sovereign in her appalling inhumanity. Like clowns and spiders and anything without a proper face, the picture scared me. I wrapped it back up a second time and put it into the cupboard for the next tenant to stumble on.

All the while I was feeling vaguely ill, not quite myself. Almost someone else. I took another pregnancy test in the empty flat, and sat hopelessly on the edge of the bed. In my hands, a strong blue cross appeared.

I slept with Thee
till I grew pregnant with God's goodness

I imagine her praying. Whether she is praying the Psalms or simply conscious of God's eyes on her, whether she is kneeling or fetching water from the well, she is praying. It's impossible that she's not praying. From when she was tiny, her blood beat with consciousness of God. That is what it means to be Mary. As she prays, she hears words; she looks up. She's disturbed, but quickly steadies herself. This is a part of the prayer, she realizes, and then she's not scared. She talks back to the angel; she knows what to ask. The words sink into her. And so does God. She has the sense that all this has happened before and will happen for all time.

In the more ordinary way of things, there are days when the fertilized egg voyages along the fallopian tube, blown by the winds of cilia, to implant itself in the readied lining of a uterus. Discovering the truth of that earliest phase, those flukey days of pregnancy and nonpregnancy, or nearly pregnancy, astonished me. The moment between cup and lip, between throwing a stone and the stone breaking water. The held breath, the fraught voyage of the pierced egg to the place where it will rest for nine months, of which we know nothing. And then the days of digging in, the quiet, precarious moments of gestation before most women know they are carrying a life.

Mary did not have those blind days. She knew of that silent overshadowing. He brought her into those dark wings of time, before the action starts. She knew from the beginning. And once she knew, how did she ever move again?

Did he leave her on her knees in the courtyard? Or was she standing, perfectly still? Were her hands at her mouth or held together in prayer? How did she ever collect herself to go into the house and prepare dinner? What did she cook? How did she keep her silence?

Perhaps every day in those first weeks, she returned to the place of that meeting (in a courtyard, by a well), knelt, and listened. Perhaps she asked more questions of the implacable air. Perhaps she sensed his presence in stillness, in the moments before all this becomes as apparent as the blossom on a mimosa tree, before veins and heartbeats, kicks and wriggling. She felt, perhaps, a bit strange. Not quite herself. She absorbed the tremendousness of what was happening. And I think, because it was her, she was quickly suffused in love.

The courtyard became saturated in darkness. The sun rose, set, the streets darkened again. She lay awake alone on her bed and knew God on her, with her, over her, in her, like water. There was, I believe (but only now, after decades of her hidden presence), no fear in her.

ନ୍ଦ

In a house close to Rome, I stood naked in the bathroom before the mirror. A bright blue map of veins was webbed through the whiteness of my chest. I'd never seen anything like it. I looked it up online to reassure myself that this was normal. It was— but I didn't think anyone else could ever have had architecture this obvious written on them. My body (usually so queasy, whiney, and gripe-prone) was doing its own thing. Watching it was like standing on a quay and beholding a clipper ship be expertly rigged: the hands of men all hidden in the workings, the wondrous unfurling of the rolled sails. Ropes and cables appeared through me even as I observed. My pelvis cranked apart like a bridge opening its bascules for something large approaching on the river. It was not without pain. I ached and moaned. No one tells you this: how, all of a sudden, the body prepares to become something far beyond itself: its blood volume will almost double, its skin will stretch impossibly. It will effortlessly look after itself and a small passenger. My body was having its day.

There was only a little nausea. (I'd suffered worse on car rides, before dates, after dates.) In our new house, Fabio was busy spraying beeswax polish on all the doors and cupboards. It made me sicker. I sucked on lemon ice lollies and inhaled the new sea air and the scent of blue rosemary that was planted all down the shoreline.

Hundreds of thousands of times, I'd seen Mary on her own cusp of motherhood. At the Annunciation, artists have her kneeling (Caravaggio), bowing (Lippi), hands raised as if to protect herself from a blow (Botticelli), hands clasped in prayer (Reni), regal (Leonardo), stricken (Waterhouse), mildly curious (Crivelli), intense (Hacker), humble (Tanner), blank (Fra Angelico), shocked (Koninck), and nonplussed (Collier). They say that she was troubled at the sight of the angel, they say that she quickly calmed and took stock. They say that she, as though standing naked before a mirror and seeing her own veins raise up within her, announced herself as the "handmaid of the Lord."

"You will conceive in your womb," says the angel, as though he is the flat white stick on which the blue cross appears. Though Tertullian believed that women contributed little to the making of a child (were, in effect, a nest) and Aristotle reckoned that women were the substance and men were the catalyst—as milk is set by rennet—and it would be centuries before we understood the full role of *any* woman in all of this, I knew that Mary was involved, like me, in every single cell of her child; that her DNA would be stamped through him; that she rose up, as I did, with a creative script written into her. But a script, as believers had it, of the magnitude of the extraordinary, the exotically feathered, the impossible. Which is what I felt about my own changing body. Which is why I would (in time) be even more in awe of *her*.

As we settled into our new home by the Roman sea, I became bewitched by Yeats' poem "Leda and the Swan"—a staggering depiction of bestial rape by a god in the form of a bird, and one that must have had, I felt, similarities to the story of Mary's encounter with the angel. "The feathered glory" and "the great wings beating still" could also, I thought, belong to Gabriel. To me, back then, the two tales seemed almost parallel: a coupling of two very different beings and the explosion of an unlikely new life. Realistically, I still believed, as I had that night on the Plains, that Mary had been raped. Human tragedy had locked horns with myth and left us with a doomed mother from whom our minds and hearts would never be free.

But even then, in Mary's buried, mysterious story, I felt the brush of some fellow feeling. I thought that my questions at the start of motherhood must surely have been one hundred times hers: What kind of child was I bringing into this world? What path would we be called on to walk?

What would be asked of us?

ౙౙ

In many ways, life in this new town by the sea was a helpful distraction from the natural drama of early pregnancy. It was a strange town. A Roman bridge had been excavated in one corner, a temple to Minerva lay at the bottom of our street, and the foundations of Etruscan houses were always being unearthed. But the skyline was beset with 1960s apartment blocks and litter fermented in the gutters. Bauhaus and liberty mansions with painted tiles, glittery domes, and ornate stairwells crowded the approximate center of this settlement, which was long and thin and hugged the coastline. At the end of every short street, we were met by the immaculate blue of the sea. In the days of *La Dolce Vita*, the town had been home to film stars and writers. Now, an old Polish man lived outside the church and Filipino maids congregated on the boardwalk on Sundays. Behind the station, flats were occupied by American students who walked the beaches in the evenings, reading from books and debating loudly. St. Augustine himself landed from Africa just a little further up that coastline. Until a few years before we arrived, all the street signs in town were duplicated in Russian to welcome the tide of post-Soviet immigrants. The new incomers were Chinese, and every street corner burst with cheap supplies of everything you could think to need. Africans roamed the streets now too, selling jewelry.

The town was always a haven for "blow-ins," as the Irish call outsiders. I befriended a redheaded New Yorker named Maisie, who lighted on the seaside resort after 9/11 as a place to heal and retire. A nonbeliever with an uncanny talent for piano playing, we would sit by the fire in her basement and, over wine or whiskey, cattily critique the notions of the patriarchal Church. Then, as the street above us sunk to darkness, she would play me anything I asked for—"Every Time We Say Goodbye," "Imagine," "Greensleeves." I heard tell of a Ukrainian priest too, a man who had fled his homeland on pain of death and now ran the streets every day as if his would-be executioners were still after him. Recognizing another "blow-in," he once stopped when he saw me on the high street and checked that he knew everyone in town that I knew before running on. Anyone I had coffee with was affrighted or on their way through. Everyone had that look in their eyes that said "This is not my home—I'm waiting for the next train out." Even Maisie, who was the most content of us all, was up all night talking to New York. The place was a refuge for the wounded, displaced, uncertain, and disappointed; it was a mishmash of history and happenstance.

Mary's image could be found on walls and in niches throughout the little town. When I took the train to Rome with Fabio at weekends, her presence was more graceful than it had been on the island—but she still loomed large. A mosaic portrait of her was high above a corner of St. Peter's Square with the words *Totus Tuus* (All for You) inscribed beneath. The words seemed to express an outlandish notion. I mourned Mary of Nazareth, the girl with the interesting and untold story. At the same time, I had far fewer thoughts about her. As my belly grew, I was too busy trying to untangle the mysteries of prenatal care, in a language I hardly spoke, to understand which scans and tests were useful and which were not. There was one blood test that I felt was necessary and asked our neighbor about over the hedge. "Listen," she said, "your baby will be as the Lord Jesus wants it, whatever you do or don't do."

The idea terrified me. Fabio, on the other hand, had no truck with the future. He neither rued nor planned. This gave him little patience with those who did. Our mealtimes on our new back terrace began to follow a predictable pattern of my ruminations—ifs, thens, whens, and maybes—and his ultimate explosion. It made his head throb to consider that soon a flesh-and-blood being would be beside us at the table.

We had made our move together across the sea, but now I was beginning the long discovery that marriage itself is another country. I had believed that we would share everything in that poetic expression "one flesh"—but the fleshly boundaries were quite different. It was I to wake with an aching pelvis and to lie there, wondering at the ceiling. It was I to stammer in shops and come out with the wrong item in my bag. And now that we had firmly decided to raise our family on Fabio's linguistic territory, it was I to become the weaker, wordless partner. He was the doer; I the worrier, the self-obsessed.

One early morning, unable to sleep, I went down to the beach and watched the fishermen return from the morning catch. That hour always amazed me: the sea was pale and smooth as cream and so identical in color to the sky that the horizon was impossible to see. The boatmen in their wooden fishing boats were silhouettes as they punted with an oar back to shore. Then, as I watched them in their stillness, the baby flickered in my belly. It was a marginal sensation, but inescapable. It happened again. As light as an eyelid batting or a butterfly wing. Again, I stood back and watched as my body—and now the child's—did the moves. It was all in hand. The child danced within me as though she'd seen the script beforehand and been coached in all her acrobatics. She pulsed with knowledge, and I felt all my rangy fear leave me—at least for those minutes. I was a fortress around her, a mother ship, a sounding board, a stadium. A home.

My soul magnifies the Lord,
my spirit rejoices in God my Savior

Mary set off to her cousin's to help her in her own confinement, the child simmering in her like barely suppressed news—and her cousin's baby danced at her words, like Wisdom, like the Virgin! *It is beyond us*, I want to shout now. *It—every baby, every story—is beyond us!*

But back then, I had yet to know the truth of this.

The nights drew in and the oranges on the tree in the backyard ripened and were the most delicious I had ever tasted. They progressed from green to a mosaic of lime and yellow to orange, and were sweet without a trace of acidity. The time had almost arrived. I was booked into Gemelli, the pope's hospital, for the birth. We visited a few weeks before my due date and were shown the vast nursery of newborns.

"Why aren't they with their mothers?" I asked the nurse.

She wagged a finger at me. "No. No. Not yet. They're with specialist nurses."

"But what about breastfeeding?"

"They see their mothers every few hours."

"Could I choose to have her with me?"

The nurse wagged her finger at me again. "It's best like this."

I could see nurses giving babies bottles through the glass.

"But how can breastfeeding be established?"

She pointed to my belly with surprise: "It's very small."

And she walked off.

When Fabio returned with tea from the bar, he could not understand my collapse into despair. He could not see why the hospital might not be to my liking. I was being unreasonable. He went off to find the nurse, and I sat on a wall wondering how I could navigate something so important as *life* in another country, in a language that still foxed my tongue.

But thought and planning were stolen from me (and from the prescriptive nurse at that large hospital). One autumn evening, five days before my due date, I lost a cup-full of bright red blood, and the contractions began.

For the pain, we couldn't make it all the way to Gemelli, and once inside the walls of Rome, we careered into the *Pronto Soccorso* of a smaller hospital. As I stepped inside the building, my water broke. Having charged through the cold dark in thundering pain, I was stunned by the light, heat, and (I swear) cigarette-smoking nonchalance of the night staff. (They *can't* have been actually smoking, but they must have smelt of smoke, have had their coats on as they came in from a puff.) They leaned, they slouched, they commented and wise-cracked. *Urgent!* I wanted to yell. But of course, I had to be clerked in with a gamut of bald questions. Perhaps the baby would have shot out of me had things been different. After an hour or so of groaning, and not much else occurring, we discovered that her head was flung back and she was, in effect, stuck.

The pain rode through me. I vomited and shook. Epidural after epidural was administered but still the pain blasted on. "Your wife doesn't have a normal reaction to anesthesia," I heard the doctor tell Fabio. When they left the room, I got to my feet to go to the bathroom and my legs folded under me. Bang. Coccyx collided with floor; I bounced over and banged my head. "Mio Dio!" wailed the nurse when she ran back into the room.

She was Peruvian, the nurse, and once she had me back on the bed, and the drugs finally began to work, she rubbed my lower back and sang. I thought I could stay like that forever; in fact, I wanted to stay like that forever because the way forward involved only tearing and more pain. I wanted to hide in the doped dish of night. And we did, dozing and singing for hours. The epidurals had stopped the contractions, the baby continued to search for God in the heavens of my womb, the nurse held my hand and stroked my hair. And then, as the sun began to creep above the horizon over Rome, the Peruvian nurse collected her coat and bag and came to kiss me goodbye, and a German nurse took over, checked her clipboard and my cervix, and announced that it was time to get this baby out. I agreed, seeing the red sun and hearing *dawn*, in my poet's addled brain, and therefore "new beginnings." But there were still no contractions, and so Oxytocin was given and the pain took on another dimension.

This pain broke walls and opened horizons I never knew existed. I hallucinated black horses' hooves stampeding through me toward landscapes that had no end. I had no idea suffering like that could exist—like there was a fourth dimension I had never suspected. It had no death; it wouldn't ever stop. This thought seemed the profoundest I had ever known. You can't destroy pain. You fence it back, you drug it, you shut it up in a room, but it never dies.

Still, the baby couldn't come. More men with clipboards. No Peruvian nurse now, no hands, just a succession of people in blue scrubs observing and writing. And Fabio beside me, and not beside me, trying to arrange a way out of this.

I was being wheeled along corridors and through swing doors, Fabio behind me.

"I'm here. I'm right here. I'm here. I can't come any further. I'm right outside."

They lifted me onto the steel slab of operation, which added to the agony because agony is not straight and won't be laid flat on its back.

"Shall I put you out? Shall I finish it here?" the white-haired anesthesiologist asked me. Perhaps he spoke in English—I can't recall—but those are the words I remember, and I know I thought he was offering to kill me or to go so far with his help that I might die, and I said, "Okay."

But the next thing I knew there were screams—desperate, life-gulping screams—and they brought the baby to me and laid her cheek against my cheek. When I said her name, she stopped crying instantly, knew the voice of the womb here, now, in the acoustics of a room. "Hello, Celia Florence," I said, "What a terrible night we've had." She took this in with great attention, as though in the shelter of a great rock. And then they took her away again, to light and wind, and she howled.

Recovery was not quick. Fabio seemed to have disappeared; he was busy, I gathered, with registering the birth, going home to sleep, and organizing his parents' boat tickets and collecting them from the port. In England, my own mother was trying to buy a same-day plane ticket, and managed. She would see her granddaughter the day of her birth, twelve hours after delivery. But what I remember of the first day as a mother myself was the feeling of being an island. The other mothers were surrounded immediately by family, balloons, and fuss. They had all called their kids something modish and recognizable, like Asia or Azzura. It was possible, an Italian friend pointed out later, that the staff took me for a Romanian, and that was why I was treated with some disdain. (It was hard to feel cheered by this.) As I lay, boiling hot and still paralyzed from the waist down in the overheated room, some paper handkerchiefs fell from my bed onto the floor, but I was too drowsy to notice. When the cleaner came by she gave me a sharp lecture, scolding my filth and disrespect: "Che gente!" ("What people!") My thick tongue tried to find the words in Italian to explain that I couldn't move, but no words came. I heard the mother next to me tut and whisper to her visitors as they gave me sidelong glances.

My daughter's name, too, caused confusion. Celia is an ancient Roman name; one of the seven hills of Rome is Celio. The last vestal virgin to keep the pagan flame of Rome alight was named Celia Concordia. The name belongs with the great Roman families of Giulia, Flavia, and Lidia but has fallen out of fashion, though Ben Jonson, William Shakespeare, and George Eliot picked it up for their heroines. But the Roman cleaners said "Che vuol' di'?" with scorn—"What does it mean?"—though I heard it only in its literal translation of "What does it want to say?"

It wants to say: skies, heavenly. It wants to drink to me with thine eyes. It wants to say: *Shall we be sundered? Shall we part, sweet girl? No.* It wants to allude to *Santa Maria in Ara Coeli*, which she will one day climb up to on her sturdy little legs to see the splendid series of chandeliers and the icon of the Virgin above the altar: *Madonna Advocata*.

In those early weeks, Celia and I—like any mother and baby—were one. She perceived me as part of herself. The drama of her exit from my body was only the beginning of her untangling from me. She would have to learn that my hand was not her hand, my joy was not her joy, my voice was not her voice, though her cells would remain inside me for many years to come.

In the hospital, we snuggled in bed, shutting out the lights and noise around us. The mother next to me was on her second child. She was on first-name terms with the cleaners and nurses and knew what she was doing. On the other side, a teenage girl was having a mysterious intervention. There were many tears and whispers. I don't believe that any of us exchanged a word. Perhaps I did not have the language or was too drugged. If we did speak, the words did not penetrate the new reality of being with this other person who came with me down into the pit of the birth and its immediate aftermath.

Celia was the only person who *could* have accompanied me down to that pit—even if they had let Fabio through the operating theater door. Birth partners are wonderful, I hear, and bring all kinds of benefits. But you only go beyond the edge, where limits to suffering dissolve, with the child who is so definitively entwined with you. They say that Mary gave birth without pain, and who am I to say otherwise. But in the courtyard of the Annunciation, and even in the grotto of the birth, Mary was alone. No one, not even her husband, could possibly imagine what was happening to her. "Alone of all your sex," Sedulius wrote, and the feminists seized on this as example of the Virgin's difference, her exceptionality, her exceptional holiness, her exceptional loneliness—her special subordination to God and man. Mary, alone. But what I will arrive at, in a shortening number of days, is Mary's aloneness as the archetype of *every* woman's aloneness: Mary as foundress, as defender, as mother-creator, as collider with the harsh, existing world. For, in childbirth, there is no act of creation so similar to God's as he pulled form out of nothing and watched the world spin.

Whatever Mary's experience of giving birth, I think now, she knows what it is to be the mother of a unique story. In fact, she defines the *uniqueness* that, paradoxically, pricks every woman as she brings a unique being into the world. She knows that only her own child can look into her eyes and *know* what she went through. Only her own child can share in that companionable aloneness. Only the child—who is, for Mary, God himself.

When I looked at Piero della Francesca's *Madonna del Parto* years after I gave birth, I thought I saw another error in how we portray the Virgin. There is extraordinary pride in Mary in that painting. She has a raised, Florentine chin. One hand rests nonchalantly on a hip, and the other draws aside her blue dress as if to reveal not a bump but a sword or a gun. Beyond her, the angels stand to each side, like stagehands pulling apart the curtains of a scene, evoking, of course, the tearing of the temple veil, the ending, the beginning of everything. But look into the gaze of Mary's brown eyes: only God can enter there.

※

"Let her fall!" The woman's voice was half sing-song provocation, half battle cry: "Let her fall!"

The mothers on the promenade let forth a rumble of agreement, or turned away. The woman was marching up to me now. I thought: she's not a mamma, she's a nonna (a grandmother). Her face was creased, and her eyes were dulled like a pencil by years of pressing her point. But her hair was streaked green at the front, and she stabbed at the air with a cigarette.

When she saw my face, she rattled out a cigarettey laugh: "She's beautiful." We watched my daughter—on her feet again now—hurtle down the boardwalk with violet fairy's wings strapped to her back. "But you have to let her fall. No pick up." She passed into choppy English now that she had the measure of me. "You want coffee?" I shook my head and felt stupid tears pile up at the back of my eyes. It was carnival, and the ground was thick with chucked confetti. In the purple dusk, the sea was breaking more than usual. Rain began to hit the debris and wind swept up streamers. The mothers shrieked and hassled their children into cars. I heard my daughter laugh as she ran right down the boardwalk. "Che fai? Che fai?" ("What are you doing?" I must have heard it in my head because the storm canceled everything else but Celia laughing.) "You'll catch pneumonia!" the nonna with the green hair yelled from a car window as she sped past. Celia and I put our faces up to a sky the color of fresh bruises and tried to catch the rain on our tongues.

It was true that I could not let my daughter fall—or, anyway, not pick her up. I had the reputation in the playground of being the overprotective one. You had (the consensus seemed to be) to play roulette with the unfenced play area that bordered a road, or at least with the top of the climbing frame, to toughen a child for the season of their life. At the same time, here, you could not let your child sweat when they ran. By the coffee bar, by the slides, there was even a bank of hairdryers that the mammas used to dry off their hectic, slippery kids. "Non sudare!" ("Don't sweat!") was the most shouted instruction through those afternoons. (The mornings did not exist. They were English time, I discovered, when the Italians were doing other things, and we had the shady park to ourselves.)

And, of course, she fell. Down a stone step outside a coffee bar, her satin knee was grazed for the first time. "Oh!" She jumped up and, after a momentary wince in my arms, trotted off to be with her friends. But I stood there, some pain piercing me deeper than I knew I had depths. "Are you okay?" a new American friend asked, touching my arm. It felt like ancestral pain, some weird opening into both history and possibility. The tears spilled.

"It's just hormones."

She agreed and laughed, and we drank our coffee. But as we walked home, I almost despaired of the thin line between my daughter and myself. Her hurts blossomed within me. Her hunger, her thirst, her distress were like roars in an empty room. They shook the walls of my heart so I no longer knew what was sound and what was me—like the bloody man-God on the cross, I would think years later, who takes on all of our wounds and sins with no limit. I knew already that maternal empathy was something extraordinary. I was approaching the discovery that it is almost divine.

And I came upon Mary again, for the first time since the Lippi, since Guadalupe. I came across her in memory, in the visceral compassion of my motherhood, in that time of my hands being my child's hands, and her face being my face, in the long shadow of Signora Angelica and her grief.

We had toured, so many times, the churches and ruins of Rome, explaining history and artwork to friends from England and America and consuming countless dishes of *amatriciana* and glasses of *limoncello*. Of all the artworks that I remembered in the Basilica of St. Peter, this was the quietest, the most otherworldly. Kept behind glass now, like a great flower walled in silence, Michelangelo called this his *capolavoro*. He even signed his name on the sash across Mary's breast. (He never signed another work of art.)

In this, the heart's image, mother and son are one marble pyramid, her head the vertex, the rock of Golgotha the base. Despite the realism—the muscles, the fingernails, the veil—Mary, here, is disproportionately large: no normal-sized woman could cradle her dead son that way. Jesus has given up the ghost; his face is bloodless and serene. And this outsized Virgin is the receiving world. Her arms and fingers are long and tapered as branches that seem to have caught him in a precipitous fall from on high. In Robert Hupka's photograph of this masterpiece, taken from above, this sheer fall is captured: we see that Christ has descended, plumb as a stone dropped into a lake or an orange from a tree to the earth.

As we walk around them, this entwined mother and son, we see that the Virgin's hands say two things: one catches him, grasps him, possesses him—knows that, without her, he will fall from the knowable world. But the left hand gestures, *What is this?* It is this hand that speaks to God, like Esther's plea ("Help me, who am alone and have no helper but you"); like Job's lament ("Why is light given to one in misery?"); and like her own song ("My soul magnifies the Lord . . ."). The left hand says *This*—meaning, this is everything: all love, all sacrifice, all pain. All question and all answer.

Yes, her lap is wide; she can take anything: the world, the world's sorrow. Even—though at such cost—*him*. This scene is the interface of God's pain and the world's rage, the world's pain and God's rage, God's love and the world's need, the world's love and God choosing, heart-wrenchingly, to need. It is an intolerable sight cast in marble. It is the only sight.

Almost forty years before I would see it, a man arrived in Rome with a hammer and attacked it, breaking off Mary's arm, her nose, and an eyelid. The random man with the hammer tried to undo all of it. It was too much. "Each man kills the thing he loves." One hundred pieces of her break off and are shattered on the floor. The left arm—the declaiming, signaling arm—falls. The tourists scream. A man grabs the beard of the attacker and flings him away. People scramble to gather bits of her, to save, to steal. In the days and weeks that follow, one of those parts is returned as though from a kidnapper, and, through minuscule reconstruction of all the shattered fragments, she is somewhat given back to herself (as Christ restored her after the Resurrection in St. Teresa's vision). Some features cannot be saved. Her beautiful nose is pieced painstakingly together, but new parts have to be grafted on from the dust of Carrara marble, as though she is a burns patient receiving new skin. So when I come to know her, she is whole again, but behind glass, gesturing to his dead body with her reconstituted left hand as if there are no words, signing the unspeakable.

I stood in front of that statue in what I did not know was prayer. And as I cradled my daughter when she was ill, when she suffered, Mary's form overshadowed me again, as it had in the gallery in London, as it did in the Midwestern blizzard and *S'Incontru* on the island. Now she seemed to hug my shape like a mold.

By looking at this statue, we learn how to stand under the cross. How not to run away. Almost a decade later, a novel will be published imagining that Mary (whose quintessence is compassion: *cum patior*, I suffer with) *does* run away. I would read the back cover of this lauded novel as I stood in a bookshop in London, many years after giving birth. I had heard about the book. It was supposed to challenge everything we think we know about Mary, present her as a woman fed up with her crazy messianic son, unbelieving, and very much afraid for her own hide. I slid the copy back onto the shelf and thought: this man not only understands little of Mary; he understands little of any mother. In the years to come I have, I admit, wondered about that book. Fellow writers will remind me that artists must have the freedom to reinterpret and to imagine. Isn't it healthy to consider that Mary would have been frightened, conflicted? It is, of course. But the novel might, like Ofili's elephant dung Madonna, inadvertently deface something that is, actually, more ordinary: the almost divine love of the countless mothers who do not walk away, who do not doubt their children, and who have always been exemplified and perfected in Mary. But, of course, the book defaces more than this. The genius of the faith is that God took on the world's pain himself—but without the compassionate witness of the mother, a whole human dimension would be lost. She is the altar of sacrifice, the tabernacle of his being, the ears for his cries, the eyes for his wounds. The element of the Woman is essential.

And she was watching me. I know now that she was walking with me. My daughter fell, picked herself up, and ran again, bouncing into a spring that was the most radiant I had ever seen. We were both hungry for discovery, for knowledge, and as my hand became distinct from her hand, and my eyes lifted from hers, we hurtled into changes that were making Mary smile, that I could never have dreamed.

The Statue of Our Lady of Walsingham,
1922, commissioned by Fr. Alfred Hope Patten, based on
the medieval seal of Walsingham Priory

FOUR

The Answering Call

i

And the Word became flesh

Years later, I was sitting on a bench, at the end of a day away from home, looking down at riverboats of tourists wending their way south in the dusk and a fisherman casting off from a stone island. Celia was still little enough to need me in her routine. I worked all morning while she was in school and then, together, we tackled the mysteries of Italian homework or attended one of the many birthday parties in colorful padded rooms. But occasionally I managed to come into the city alone to buy a book or to meet a friend for lunch. Sometimes I would just journey through the city on foot, letting my unusual solitude—and the muscular stone angels, the domes and green river—sink in. The walls of the riverbank where I sat that day were covered in mold and the black of pollution. But someone, in reverse graffiti, had artfully scraped away shapes and lines in the dark dust to create larger-than-life murals. It wasn't a picture of Mary to emerge this time but instead a wolf, angels, and soldiers.

Oddly, I didn't miss Mary.

But if she could have looked into my heart (and perhaps, by the grace of God, she did), she would have seen another face as dark as that dust along the riverbank. A long face with deep eyes, swaths of bloody, tangled hair, and a crown of thorns. The glints and lights that showed the shape of this face were all him. The darkness on which he imprinted his image was myself. The coexistence of this light and dark—like the dust and scraped-clean wall of those graffiti images—were what revealed him to me—somehow, mysteriously—within myself.

I was Catholic. This event, this spectacular *volte-face*, had caused uproar in my family and lost me some friends. I had betrayed myself, they said, betrayed my feminism, my intellect, and my liberty. My uncle back in London had quit the smokes and even the drink—which meant that the two of us avoided a boozy row. But he was still in a blazing fury about my new beliefs. Only one poet from the old London years wrote to say that he was not surprised: the seeds of my conversion had all been there, in my poems. How many times had I spoken of Mary?

It was strange that, as I ambled from church to church in those days in Rome, I wasn't looking for pictures of the Virgin anymore. But I couldn't help but see her. How could I go into the church of Sant'Agostino without standing before Caravaggio's *La Madonna dei Pellegrini*? The painting was all about light: first of all, the light of the artfully positioned lamps in the church, and then the *chiaroscuro*, which accentuates flesh and the crumpled folds of Mary's scarlet and dark blue dress. Caravaggio's Mary is drowsy, lithe, and strong. She crosses her legs as she stands to let one thigh take the weight of a little boy who must, judging by his size, be two years old. He is grinning, pink, and fresh from the bath. She is inscrutable as a Roman goddess. I loved the art, but I didn't recognize Mary.

I sometimes visited the lavish golden ceiling of Santa Maria Maggiore, and when I did I couldn't help but see the serious and unglamorous brow of *Salus Populi Romani* (Mary's portrait painted, they say, by St. Luke). And when I stopped for confession in the voluptuous gold of La Chiesa del Gesù, I had to pause at *La Madonna della Strada* to see Mary's coy face surrounded by charcoal and brown.

Outside in the streets, other faces patterned the city. There was a pilgrim with dreadlocks shouting to the whole riveted piazza "Jesus is coming! Jesus is coming!" The slick *carabinieri* removing his white gloves with his teeth before taking a coffee from a scuttling barista who ran back inside, holding his tray on his head. The African street-sellers in long cotton robes with their rows of Gucci bags. Tourists with their unblinking gazes following a high flag on a stick. And the tired and serious pilgrims, whose eyes were fixed on a cluttered horizon.

As I walked to Mass, there was the stench of men and women in sleeping bags, dreaming their own truncated stories. Sometimes, I knelt down to talk with them: Jonah had come from Albania and pleaded with me to pray for his parents. Agnes was from Peru and seemed drugged. Michele had arrived two years before from Bosnia, full of reckless hope that was turning to rot. His face had lost its clean definition, as though the beard that he could not keep down was a weed, choking the determined young man he had been.

Beyond the colonnades of St. Peter's, in an underpass full of blankets and bodies, a woman with long black hair played an accordion while a little girl, with a very old face, danced. "Don't give them money," the mammas at the school gate would say, "it goes into the pockets of organized crime." (*If anyone wants to take your coat, give your cloak as well.*)

Among the gold ceilings and mosaics, art and statues there was filth, urine, spilled soda, dropped burger, and human flesh against cold stone.

"Pray for the people back home," Jonah always said when I left him after a few minutes' paltry conversation, as though he was, somehow, more fortunate on his voyage than they.

At 7 p.m., after Mass at a church near San Pietro, a man stood holding out a cloth cap for change. I knew him. I recognized his very blue eyes and his crooked ankles that made walking a struggle. Beggars sat at most church doors in Rome and often wailed. They were often fulsome women in black, lamenting the fact of hungry children at home. This man was quiet, even gentle. Back in the town where we both lived, he took off his cap and ran his hands through his hair to tidy it before receiving Communion. One spring evening, I had seen him outside a church in another town. And now here, today, far from home.

"How did you get here? How will you get back?" I asked him, wondering if I would risk too much if I offered him my arm to the station.

(*Who is my neighbor?*)

"My moped," he nodded, gesturing to the vacant street behind him. And I nodded with stupid relief and went on my way.

But only as far as the bench by the river. It had been years now since my conversion. Years since one evening, sitting on my bed, I'd put a book down and *considered* (meaning, some say, with the stars, reflecting with the aid of the stars, navigating by a star) that there could be a God, that I could have been purposefully created by him, and was filled with careful wonder in every cell.

It had been years since I discovered that face within me, a face that seemed less painted, even in this city, than that of his mother. In San Paolo and Santi Cosma e Damiano, the eyes of Christ followed me everywhere. But in so many churches, it was a portrait of Mary that sat above the altar. Even in my own home, Mary's face outnumbered his: we only kept one icon of Christ on a high shelf. His was a face that swallowed my attention whole. If I surrounded myself with those eyes, I wouldn't be able to walk a straight line to the kitchen. Kneeling before the tabernacle after Mass, I had the sensation of my face being pulled to that face, as though I were one of two lovers on the threshold of a kiss—that moment when flesh is millimeters from flesh, and the hairs of the skin, two auras of electricity, have engaged, and are drawing you in.

This is why I became Catholic, I told people who asked. I had—almost by accident in a little church one day—encountered this Presence: the Word made Flesh and ready to be consumed. When he came to me that day, every image and element of my life, all of its infinitesimal pixels, cohered into a whole before him and was suffused with his love; he who, when I became Catholic, would be physically, not just within grasp, but within me.

My Lord and my God

On the way back home, the city's faces flickered in my head to the lazy beat of the train. I was going back to small-town noise and the general hush of the sea. Sometimes I would lie awake, knowing the face of Christ inside me, and the faces of others—those I'd upset and hurt, those I loved or ignored, the beggars and the helpless, the ranks of tourists, Jonah, Agnes, Emmaus who begged outside the supermarket—and wanting to reach out my hand and say "No" or "I'm here." But I spoke, instead, Christ's name into the darkness.

For a long time, I believed that Mary led me into this strange Body that is the Church, to the real food of God. Then simply disappeared.

There is no new revelation after Christ

֍

When summer came, the few homeless of our town took to sleeping on the beach. The Ukrainian priest said he saw them unfolding from empty changing huts as dawn broke. If he was praying his Psalms on the boardwalk before sunrise, he saw the occasional bundled body asleep on the sand.

It was the exiled Ukrainian priest who ran the streets of Santa Marinella who had prepared me for my entrance into the Church. He now rented rooms in the center of town and celebrated Divine Liturgy in a little church with a golden dome by the castle. Sometimes, once I had dropped Celia at school, I would walk across the piazza with him and talk on the porch before he began celebrating. He knew the faith. He also knew Greek and Latin, plus Ukrainian, Italian, some Russian, and French. I trusted him to read whatever I wrote in those early days; if there was a shred of theological error in a poem, he saw it, and I saw it too once it was pointed out, because bad theology, I discovered, made for bad poetry.

This priest was a fastidious and studious man whose Slavic black eyes tucked away all he heard and ticked with benign humor. He knew everything about the people of the town from his daily perambulations around the bakery, newsagent, bar, and supermarket. If there was a rumor of a child being slapped in one of the schools, he would gather the relevant information from the mother of three who owned the fabric shop on the corner and hand it on to me. Like Dickens, one of his favorite authors, he missed nothing, and found humanity and humor in almost everyone.

There was a Sacred Heart painting in the side aisle of the little church, and one day, when I attended liturgy, the priest preached about the Byzantine devotion to the Lover of Mankind. On that ordinary Thursday, my friend and I had come, he told us, like the women with the oil on Easter Sunday. We had stepped outside our working day, like Veronica with her cloth. Our acts of weekday devotion were small, but indelible in the mind of God.

I trusted this priest. But I found his devotion to the Theotokos—the Mother of God—frankly disproportionate. There were so many icons, so much bowing, so many prayers.

"But when you pray, where *is* Mary?" I asked him as we crossed the piazza one morning. The baker was taking bread out of the ovens, and the priest stopped to buy a loaf for his lunch. "Isn't she *between* you and Jesus?" I nagged as we crossed a road and he waved to the haberdasher.

"No." He unlocked the thick wooden door. Inside, an orange shaft of morning light from a stained glass window lit the altar.

"So, where is she?"

"She's with me."

He lit the candles in the freezing church and put on his vestments.

I would have no more time for questions until the end of liturgy when he sat beside me on a wooden pew.

"The Theotokos isn't simply a woman. She's a *place*. The holy city. She's the womb that encompasses you and Christ—you're both within her. You pray within her, and in that holding-space, you become closer to him."

"But I'm as close as I can be to Christ when I receive the Eucharist."

He smiled. "Yes, you are. But loving her means more of him, not less. We become what we love and who we follow. Mary is closer than anyone else to God. He wants you to love her so that you consent to being as open as possible to his grace—like her."

He turned to me again as he put his books into his bag. "Do you think you and your family will visit *La Madonnina* anytime, and if you do, could I hitch a ride?"

La Madonnina was a statue of Mary a few miles up the road from our house that had famously wept tears of blood.

I replied bluntly that we would not be going, and stepped out into the cold sunshine.

ᔕᔕ

I never would have gone by choice.

But I had made another new friend, another "blow-in" to the town: Monica from Turin. She was a convert too, of sorts. Raised a Catholic, she had found God again when her father died. Just after my own conversion, she came up to me at one of the many birthday parties, touched the cross at my neck, and asked, "Do you wear it for a reason?" After that, we were, for many years, twin families. Our husbands were both irreligious and wouldn't come with us to Mass. My conversion, for Fabio, was still a shock, almost an infidelity. It was a relief to him to laugh with Monica's husband, who was also left alone on Sunday mornings. Our daughters were the same age, both dark-eyed, and often mistaken for sisters. Over the years, we sat beside swimming pools, at freezing pony trials, or in ballet studios, watching the girls. At weekends we ate swordfish or marinated pork on our back terrace and downed bottles of Sicilian wine.

I don't remember why we went there. Perhaps it was a stop-off on the way to the beach. We probably pulled in so that the men could have one last coffee before the long day ahead and the girls could use the bathroom. Outside the church was a big truck full of statues and rosaries, and a bar. As the girls ran around the garden, Monica and I stepped into the quaint stone church to see yet another statue of Mary.

The statue itself was surprisingly small, entirely white, and positioned discreetly to the side of the altar behind glass. Beside it were magnified photographs, taken at the time of the crying, of the figurine's bloodied cheeks.

Like everybody in the town, I knew the story, more or less. There was an ordinary family with an ordinary garden, and, as is so common in Italy, there was a statue of Mary planted in a rockery. It had been brought to the family as a gift from Medjugorje by the parish priest. That particular afternoon, the dad walked by this little statue with his daughter, and crossed himself, as he began locking up to go to evening Mass. There was nothing to see. But the little girl returned to Our Lady, for no reason she could explain—and saw red liquid ooze and pour from the statue's right eye and down its white plaster cheek. The little girl fled inside to tell her father, who, at the word *blood* rushed out, saw the statue, checked his daughter's hands for injury, and gave her a slap on the behind. But at that point a tear of blood trickled from the statue's left eye too. Stunned, the father ushered his family off to church.

That was only the first weeping. Soon, the garden was full of the devout and curious. The happenings became a major event, with the police involved and the statue taken to be locked up and examined. The bishop did not really believe any of this until, one day, he held the thing in his own hands—and it wept large tears of blood again. In Italy, they take these things seriously. The figurine had already been scanned by a team of experts from the best hospitals in Rome: there was nothing out of the ordinary. The blood was examined: it was human, male— of Jesus Christ, devotees of the statue suggested. Theories and counter-theories abounded. The family maintained that they saw apparitions of the Virgin and heard messages from her over the time to come. She spoke to them of the urgency of prayer, of conversion. She warned of war and disaster as she did in Kibeho.

I couldn't pray before this small figurine. I was grateful that the focal point of the church was the altar and not this. Monica and I stood together in silence staring at *La Madonnina* until she squeezed my hand, crossed herself, and drifted out for coffee. But I stayed some moments longer looking at the statue, thinking this would never happen in England. At least, not these days, not now. This florid thing, this strange "proof," only distanced Mary further from me. The bloody face was like something from a horror film. This alleged miracle seemed tawdry, a million miles from Jesus walking on water or the feeding of the hungry crowds. For me, the bleeding statue only raised questions.

By now, I was used to the ordinary theater of the Church (not the sacrifice of the Mass, which was the epitome of lucent understatement, as though the atom were split at the altar each day and we simply crossed ourselves and bowed our heads). I mean the theater of the tiny skull of St. Agnes in Rome, which we took our visitors to see. I mean the black tongue of St. Anthony in Padua. Or the incorrupt body of a blessed nun that lay in a glass coffin in a chapel near our house. I mean the one silver hair belonging to the head of Pope St. John Paul II that was twisted artfully around silver pins to form a flower and given to a friend. The night I was received into the Church, I was passed that saint's rosary by his housekeeper and held it in my hands. I prayed with a fragment of St. Bernadette's habit and a clump of soil from the grave of St. Rafqa. Even Mary's veil is supposedly preserved in a church in France. I had looked at its image and wondered if it had really touched her head, if her eyes had studied with pleasure its pale weave of stripes.

"It's a death cult," my New Yorker friend Maisie said of the Church, and I agreed that attachment to bodies, and things of the dead, was strange. But as a young woman, had I not gasped at the drafts of Sylvia Plath's poems in the British Library, the red-inked flower she doodled under a poem? I thought I could see her movement, her life, in each stroke—like the dried pulse of spilled blood on *La Madonnina*'s plaster cheek. (And when I walked into a hospital office a year after splitting with Mischa and saw a note in his handwriting on a file, didn't I jump violently as if it were a coiled snake?)

Yes, I had made my peace with relics, and things of the dead, with the strange shows of Catholicism. I understood them in my gut. But this statue was not a relic. It was said to speak for Mary.

That afternoon in the church, it seemed to me, an erstwhile secular feminist with a fascination for Mary of Nazareth, that humanity could be borderline abusive of this woman. Whatever the truth of *La Madonnina*, the figure of the Virgin had indisputably been hauled around by all of us for our own motives through the ages. She had been dressed up (as Italian Renaissance lady, as pioneer) and words put in her mouth (for, surely, of the thousands of Marian apparitions that continue to be reported, not all are genuine). During processions in the south of Italy, statues of Mary were even made to bow to the houses of Mafia bosses. We made of her a doll with positionable limbs. In their echoing absence, women, it seemed to me, could be even more easily exploited and abused. I thought of processions on the island on the Feast of the Assumption, which celebrated Mary's bodily transportation to heaven. They paraded a life-size doll of her with long blonde hair (*blonde* hair!) inside a glass coffin, like Sleeping Beauty. In turn, I thought of Elizabeth Siddal, the model of Dante Alighieri's Beatrice that had once seemed so like Mary to me, and how, seven years after her death on February 11, 1862, her artist-husband Dante Gabriel Rossetti paid men to go to Highgate Cemetery in the dead of night to dig up her grave.

He wanted to retrieve the manuscript of his poems that he had laid in with her as an act of repentance. He had not looked after her during her illness. There had been a mistress. But the poet's single-minded possessiveness of his work won through, and he paid four men to get back what was his.

Highgate Cemetery is as ornate, deep, and well laid out as Dante Alighieri's afterlife. There are wide, clean avenues for the rich and well-known. There are darker, tangled regions for the forgotten. Almost every grave is testimony to the character or talents of its inhabitant: a stone grand piano adorns one, angels grieve and witty words abound. But much is drowned in ivy and moss. That night, the men lit a giant bonfire to illuminate their work and to burn whatever might be contaminated. No one spoke of or recorded the act of lifting the coffin lid. Nor did they report on the stench that must have raced out of it like a long cooped-up dog. No one recorded the state of Elizabeth's face. The manuscript was worm-eaten and soft. But Lizzie! they told Rossetti (who had wisely stayed at home), Lizzie was "perfect." Only her long, red-gold hair was changed. It had grown beyond measure: it filled the coffin, and it, with the fire, made the cemetery blaze.

I was sick of gothic stories, the pain, the blood; women as the objects of our hungry, orphaned gaze. They only seemed to underline the impassability of the boundary between life and death. Elizabeth Siddal had to be as worm-eaten as the manuscript pages Rossetti received from the hands of the doctor he paid to retrieve them. The beautiful model killed herself on February 11. It was 101 years later to the day that the poet Sylvia Plath put her children to bed and gassed herself in the oven. And don't we reach into her grave, too, for her poems, for anything, anything she might have written, done, or said—the doodles, even a lock of her hair? On that same day, four years before Elizabeth's death, and 105 before Sylvia's, Mary herself appeared to a child in the south of France. The date, *February 11*, shouted at me from a page of scribbled poems on my desk at home, but I could make no sense of that coincidence.

I had no trouble believing that Mary was body and soul in heaven. But were we not (like Rossetti and his robber gang) constantly reaching through the veil between life and death to grasp at what is inaccessible? Were we just children selfishly manipulating the truth of the absent? Were we weavers of legends?

And yet I was torn, standing before this statue, for there were those occasions when Mary pushed her hand through that veil, and these weird appearances struck at the heart with the authenticity of electric shock. What child could imagine the visitation of the woman who appeared by the French rubbish dump with her light brown hair and girdle of blue; her odd demands that Bernadette drink from a fountain that did not seem to be there? A woman who said things that the uneducated Bernadette could never have dreamed up.

It seemed that Mary acted like a kind of triage nurse in the hinterland between heaven and earth, speeding some closer to God, dispensing mercy, appearing and disappearing at apposite moments in history. From Zaragoza to Rome to who-knows-where, it had been a millennia-long curtain call. Christ himself appeared in visions to Faustina, Margaret Mary Alacoque, and Sister Mary of St. Peter. But Mary appeared, so often, to children: to this fourteen-year-old French girl at Lourdes who Mary taught to cross herself with feeling, with no trace of carelessness ("as one takes the hand of a child and guides it"); to shepherd children of seven, nine, and ten, to whom she—scandalously—showed a vision of hell; to a fourteen-year-old and eleven-year-old in the Alps before whom she wept, as this statue before me was said to have wept. (And, I thought as I stood before that bleeding Madonna: Mary's tears are as crucial as her joy. They express what we should always be feeling about Christ's Passion. "I wish I could always weep like that," a Desert Father said as he came out of ecstatic prayer in which he had seen Mary by the cross.) Essentially, Mary, who laughed at Lourdes and cried at La Salette, came to where these children worked and played. She spoke their language. She understands home, roots, and how important these are to us. She knows that we all sit by strange rivers and weep. We need familiarity. Her messages are still arriving, and there is never any shortage of people who claim that they see her or speak with her—at Garabandal, Medjugorje, Bavaria, Zeitoun, Seville, Laus. Our Lady, who meets us in our earthly exile, bleeds through the veil, through the centuries, around the globe, and back again. Or do we animate the unconscious so deeply that we conjure her? Is it just that we cannot bear death and endings? Is it just that we yearn for a mother?

I stood before *La Madonnina* who had wept blood and wondered if, somehow, she spoke for Mary—if all of this could be true. But enough, I said, as I turned to the altar and the tabernacle above it. Fundamentally, it hardly mattered. This odd artifact, even these engaging stories of Marian apparitions, had nothing to do with the Creed we recited as one on Sundays. They had nothing to do with my new faith and the seriousness of giving my shirt as well as my cloak (my failure to do so causing me much perturbation). Outside, Monica was gathering the children into the car, and we drove up into the dunes for lunch in the wind and glittering sand.

"There is no more revelation after Christ," I told the Ukrainian priest over the phone some days later. I was angry about the statue, angry about talk of consecration to Mary. I wanted nothing more than Jesus. "I can't pray the Rosary anymore. It takes too long. My mind wanders." And the priest said nothing, but sighed. On the phone his sigh was like a gathering wind beginning a long way away but with all the heat and strength to gather power over acres and deserted miles of prairie, sea, and land; it lifted up paper, tin cans, branches in its path; it stirred boats on the sea and flooded harbors; it dimmed lights and guttered banks of votive candles in abandoned churches; it threatened to spin in on itself and become a hurricane.

"Okay," he said.

Do not gaze at me because I am dark,
because the sun has gazed on me

When I couldn't sleep, I went downstairs so I didn't wake Fabio with my restlessness. I lay on the settee and, in the well of stair light that was left on for our daughter, I meditated on a painting of Mary on the wall, a copy of Raphael's *Madonna del Granduca*. The background was black as a starless, moonless night, and her flesh seemed to be lit, like (I knew it by then) a jar of olive oil. The folds of her cinnamon dress and the transparency of her veil were almost impossibly realistic. The artist who painted this copy even captured the shape of the thought that hovered in her eyes (and, by then, I was awed). I knew this painting long before I knew the original that hangs in the Uffizi, and when I compared the two I couldn't help feeling that in this copy, which I passed every day, which I gazed on in sleepless nights, there was more depth and tenderness in Mary's eyes. More light.

The will of God was something that I meditated on as I watched the absorbed expression in her eyes. It was a new phenomenon to consider. In the early days of my conversion, prayer seemed like a simple falling in the strength of God's wind—traveling, almost flying, in his direction. The will of God was something that the black-robed priest spoke about a lot. Fabio had been living, too, in this will, that was like a wind. He would tell baristas and dinner party guests about how much I'd changed. Where was the argumentative feminist he first saw in a garden in London, surrounded by people? Where was the woman who would argue with him and lock him out of the house? God had silently rearranged her.

You shall know the truth and the truth shall make you odd

The neighbors listened to Fabio's concerns. They congregated in the parking lot and looked sideways up at my window. The neighborhood liked to normalize. It didn't like people doing things at different times (the park in the morning, bed at ten in summer) or going to church on weekdays. It didn't like you talking to homeless people or having coffee with a priest. The neighborhood worked against the kind of feelings that broke the norm. It worked against the foreign, like flesh on a thorn.

That spring, the corners of our garden were tangled with weeds, cobwebs, and lost tennis balls. We couldn't make anything grow on purpose, though passion flowers burst unbidden out of a hedge and honeysuckle emerged on a fence. By brutal comparison, our neighbors' gardens were pin-neat: concreted over, or the lawn so watered and tended it was like a bowling green. The neighbors' flowers were bright and unkillable, and their trees were heavy with fruit. I kept saying I would tidy our yard and plant vegetables, but it never happened.

"Why have I found favor in your sight, that you should take notice of me, when I am a foreigner?" The Ukrainian priest sent me those words from the book of Ruth, with a line that Ruth was a "type" of Mary. (As were Queen Esther who saved the Jews, and Judith who sawed the head off Holofernes. To be Catholic, it seemed, you had to see Mary everywhere.) I heard an echo of the Annunciation in the quotation ("Do not be afraid, Mary, for you have found favor with God"), but I found the widow-Ruth's basis for being a foreigner in the first place—devotion to her mother-in-law—bewildering. The soil I hacked into was hard and unpromising; the will of God suddenly undecipherable and harsh. In reply to the priest, I could only send back:

If I should die, think only this of me:
That there's some corner of a foreign field
That is forever England

"She's very English, your daughter, but we'll Italianize her, don't worry," Celia's new schoolteacher told me one afternoon at the school gate with a hard wink.

"Of course she's too English!" shouted Fabio as he walked into the kitchen, just as Big Ben chimed an hour earlier over the radio. "It's like living in the British Embassy in this house!" I had abandoned baking cakes from home when I realized that Italian ingredients coupled with British recipes made for dense, flat sponges. But now I was back to slow-cooked casseroles, full English breakfasts, mustard, bangers, and mash.

It wasn't only the aroma of eggs and bacon that filled our house. The English I wrote and spoke to my daughter was more vivid and natural to me than my awkward mix of Roman slang and formal Italian. If I spoke the language too much, it affected my written lexicon: my word choices became sophisticated and Latinate. Celia and I never spoke in Italian; she refused to use it with me. When, one day, she telephoned from school in her father-tongue to tell me she had a headache, I answered abruptly,

"Bimba, hai sbagliato numero!" ("Little girl, you've got the wrong number!")

And she had to stage-whisper, "Mum! It's me!"

No one tells you that moving to a different country presents you with stark choices: you either become a different person, sculpted by the character of another language and culture and leave behind the needs of old friends and family, or you live in a diluted world of otherness, where you are always half-understood and your suitcase is always packed.

I wasn't writing poetry. If I wrote a poem, it belonged to one moment in one mind: my own. My conversion had bled into everything about me—especially what I wrote. My old publisher was not interested in my verse now that it spoke about God. No one in the town understood anything I wrote. "If only I could read it!" Monica would say sincerely if I published anything. But the loud, abundant lunches we shared with our families on our terrace were more pressing than anything else we had to talk about. Yet if we write, if we're honest, we need to be read. Like the luthier's cello that means little until it finds a cellist, the poem does not live until it finds its listener.

Even Monica, who had a liking for the different and the odd, was impatient with my Italian, which was still pitted with error. She offered me lessons and warned me that my daughter was at an age that I would embarrass her. (That point had already arrived: instead of telling the stationer that Celia had specific requirements as she agonized over which pens to choose for school, I announced to the shop that she had special needs.) Monica was right: the Italian language had the same impenetrable mist-like quality it had when I first moved to the island all those years ago. I had failed to make it cling to my personality. This was a dangerous thing. We need to be seen; we need simple reactions to ourselves, the multitude of fleeting affirmations and comprehension that strengthens who we are in a community. Otherwise, we're like the tree falling in a forest with no one to hear it. Do we even exist?

I walked back upstairs having looked long at the downcast eyes of *La Madonna del Granduca* and whispered as I slid into bed, "Would you move to England when you retire?"

"We could," Fabio said unpromisingly, the second before he was lost back to sleep.

෨෫෨

"Do we exist?"

It was a question my five-year-old daughter would ask herself as she passed *La Madonna del Granduca* in the morning, and pause, although she was late. She was supposed to be looking for her tie. "What if all this is a dream? How do I know I'm awake?" she pondered as she descended. She couldn't find her school tie, but it arrived from nowhere on her breakfast dish looking crumpled.

School was a kind of torture, but every day she rushed in brimming with hope. It seemed impossible that a room full of other children wouldn't be fun, and it often was. They had a black-market trade in broken pencil lead and a game called "ass on fire," which involved sitting on the scalding-hot radiators to see who could bear the heat the longest. The children were, often, one body of awe, terror, and giggles as the stark-heeled teacher clattered down the corridor toward them.

The little girl lived for the moments of rupture: when the fire alarm went off and they all walked slowly, hand in hand and in hysterics, into the school garden; when her friend lobbed his tomato slice onto the ceiling at lunchtime, and the cleaner came in, yelling and brandishing a broom; when the head-teacher nun hurled the naughtiest boy's school bag out of a second-floor window in rage. She rocked and cried with mirth at all of these things when she got home. But at school, she was very quiet.

One day, she was thrilled at the news that they were to put their math books away and walk down to the church for Mass. This was unusual and exceptionally good news for all the children, who grabbed a friend's hand and jabbered like monkeys. The walk seemed long. It looked familiar in spots—the charity bin for clothes on the corner of the street, the harbor at the end of the road where the ducks swam and her mother always said as she broke up the bread, "Ducks don't live in sea water. I don't get it." Seeing these landmarks from a different angle made her excited and homesick all at the same time. She wished her mum would walk by so she could wave or at least (thinking of the others, and the teachers who used the word "baby" as an insult) just look. In they went, into the church. It was different than on Sundays—fewer people, colder. Still, it was kind of a thrill to be there when she wouldn't normally be. And so much better than math.

It was 9 a.m., and the little bell rang. Most of her friends didn't go to Mass, and she was shocked at how they carried on talking and wouldn't sit still. It made her sit even stiller and listen even harder. She was trying to make them catch her composure. But there was too much for them to look at. A friend of Dani's grandmother was near the front. Statues made their heads swivel. And when the teacher hissed at them to make not one sound, it proved too much. Francesco grabbed Lorenzo's stickers from his pocket and Lorenzo punched him, and got punched back. Samuele reached in from the pew behind, just to have a pop himself. Lavinia, next to him, shrieked. The teacher hissed and shushed but was ultimately so mortified by the turning heads and the priest's expression that she ordered the children up and out, and they were marched back to the classroom in disgrace.

But one little girl, seated at the far end of a pew, was steadfastly watching the priest and blocking out the commotion. She didn't hear what the teacher said, nor did she see her friends leave. As the first reading finished she yawned, stretched, turned, and saw for the first time that her pew was empty and she was quite alone among strangers. The fear sunk deep in her chest and sent heat down to her fingers and toes. She didn't cry out; she didn't cry. For a few seconds, everything was distant: she was blind and deaf with wonder. She had no thought of leaving the church; the school was close and she could find her way, but she had never before had to find her way anywhere, and the journey back would involve crossing two roads. For the first time, she had no anchor. The world was shifting, unfixed territory, and she was in exile. People, words, statues, the sound of a car outside seemed to move in a different way, a way that was at once horrifically close and cruelly disinterested. Soon the people would leave and she would be alone in the church. How would her mother find her? The priest was intoning and lifting his arms. She wondered if he might notice her, but it seemed unlikely. She didn't cry, but her face was hot as fire. Then a forceful hand grabbed her hand and slid her out of the pew. She had no choice but to trot alongside this adult and had no thought of resisting. The woman was a nun, and she was asking which grade she was in and who was her teacher, and seeing her safely across the roads, through the gate, and up the stairs. But the worst was yet to happen. As she walked into the classroom the teacher, far from being concerned or consoling, took her to task: she hadn't been paying attention. She had fallen into the abyss of her own distraction! When I picked her up several hours later, she told me it had been the worst day of her short life.

I was incoherent, spewing bad grammar and threats. As I climbed the stairs and burst into her classroom, then the school office, I could not let it go: I thought it would haunt me forever. The chubby head-teacher nun had the forceful voice and embrace of a Neapolitan housewife. She bellowed kindly that I had no need to worry—even Jesus got left behind.

Yes, I snapped, and Mary and Joseph searched for him, *anxiously*.

And I met Mary again. But this time, not as Wisdom; not as Tower; not as an almost deified being in the pagan rituals of rural towns; not in paint nor in marble; not as a plastic doll with long hair; not as a mysterious apparition; not in tears of blood; but in one Greek word: ὀδυνώμενοι, *odunomenoi*, in suffering, in anguish, in distress—how Mary felt as she searched for her twelve-year-old son.

I hadn't even lost my little girl. Or rather, I had not known that she was lost. But I knew Mary's footsteps, as every mother must; I knew her searching in the three days of her little boy's absence. How her mouth would be formed around his name, how a cry would be tensed in her heart like a hawk with raised wings. How her body, her being, was ready to fly. Three days that would find their echo in the lapse between death and Resurrection. I knew, then, that I could not buy the image of Mary as an imperturbable doll nor inscrutable Queen. She, too, knew desperation, knew searching, knew *hunger*. In the days between conception and heaven, she knew *missing* a person.

This one Greek word of human frailty that so many plastic images of the Virgin seemed to belie told me that she *knew*. I was left with Mary as a woman who walked dusty streets. A small person who asked for her son outside a house and was ignored. A woman who occupied a chair in the temple, a place in the market, and knew worry, aloneness, and the awkwardness of difference and exile. This exile, I guessed, was not limited to that nighttime escape to Egypt and those years as outsiders. It was the exile of difference that, I thought, could never have left her: the flayed sensation of being *other*. This, I guessed, was what united us. An exile of peculiarity.

ಬಜ

The years of childhood were soon discarded at our feet. There was no more playground, nor school plays. No more riding, ballet, and swimming. We hadn't been to the boardwalk where Celia learned to walk and ride a bike in a decade. I had lived longer at this address by the sea than anywhere else in my life. My aim in doing so had been to give my daughter roots, a sense of belonging. If Mary ever appeared to her, she would know which language to speak, which signs to give. But, I pondered as I watched Celia reading *Wuthering Heights* one sweltering afternoon, what is home? The heavy scent of jasmine in May? The hush of the sea at night? The lilt of a language? Or simply a sense of being known and understood? Celia looked, now, even more a daughter of the island: long dark hair, large eyes so dark they were almost black, and a ferocious determination in her lips and jaw. She was an Italian girl—fast-talking, exacting. But though she looked like a daughter of the island, she loved the Brontës, rainclouds, and muddy walks. She wanted to go to England to study, she told me. And then, maybe, America.

We used to wait out the hottest days to walk together down to the beach at night, where we sat on a rock as she named the stars for me as they appeared. Now I walked that stretch of beach alone in the mornings and saw the rock we sat on submerged by tide. Further on was the spot where she taught me to skim pebbles. And further on still, the place I used to tell her was where the mermaids lived. On that patch of sand, the beach ran out, and the sheltered sea was the exact same silver as the sky. It made the rocks that broke the surface of the water seem to peter out somewhere at the entrance to the heavens.

Fabio and I talked of Celia's plans as we lay in bed. It was hard for Fabio not to see her wanderlust as a betrayal of her Italian self. For any Italian, the idea of children, however grown, moving away from home is intolerable: "She will forget us. She will forget who she is." He fell into an angry sleep. But I lay awake longer with the words *Where am I?* stamped through my bones. I woke in the night, hearing the sea, and wondering where I was.

And then Italy's borders closed, the shops shut, and the churches locked their doors. It was 2020, and police patrolled the streets with megaphones telling us not to leave our homes. One morning, a Tanzanian sister from the convent for whom I had done some translations called me: "Well, that's it. We're all going to die in a foreign country," she proclaimed as the conversation moved inevitably onto the virus. "You're not going to die," said Fabio when I got off the phone, "I promise." Whatever the risk, whatever the truth or otherwise of his words, the world as we knew it was ending.

But the world is always ending.

In our back garden I heard every bird: the family of magpies, blackbirds, the starlings, doves, and chaffinches. The fear, I realized as I paced the garden, finally praying the Rosary with ease, even more than once a day, was of not being able to get home. For a time, we wondered if we ever would.

"If you like, we can move to England when I retire," Fabio said wearily one day as he brought in the shopping, "But I'm not convinced you know where home is."

The pace of my worried feet carried the prayer. Up and down the garden path, up and down, bead after bead, decade after decade. At other hours, Celia and I walked and talked. She talked a thousand futures, ten thousand books she wanted to read, places she needed to live. We beat a dust track through the grass with all our walking. I had long hours to write, but I couldn't. I looked at the poems I had written in the years since my conversion and couldn't see any connection between them or any overarching voice. I walked and prayed the Rosary, and then one day I walked off the path with the rosary still in my hand and went to my desk and wrote.

Maybe around then, I began to see how Mary approached her son at Cana and told him that there was no wine. I began to see her hand on his arm.

And yet she was still quiet. After all those years, only to be guessed at.

When the others had gone to bed, I lay awake on the settee and gazed at the copy of Raphael's *Madonna del Granduca* on the staircase. This image of Mary came at the beginning, from before the beginning. It belonged to someone who was Christian but not Catholic, was painted by someone who was Christian but not Catholic, English not Italian, and in the brush strokes I was interrogating the *why* of the artist's evident devotion and love. It seemed, now, that this picture must have the answer: the anatomy of that long pull toward Mary. The picture was the doorway. To arrive at the end, we need to go backward.

To fix one's thought on her is perfect understanding

We have to go to the house in the middle of acres of flatland, which I would visit at weekends as a child. The muddy lanes we walked took us to gates where Granddad would lean, pipe clenched between his teeth, and teach me the difference between wheat and barley and how to tie sailor's knots with the belt from my coat.

"Who would want to live anywhere else?" he (who had sailed around the world several times in the Merchant Navy) would ask, sweeping his hand across the unchanging East Anglian landscape.

We walked or biked everywhere. Grandma and Granddad mounted their huge black bicycles as they freewheeled down the lane and I pedaled manically to keep up. We never went farther than the old church of Saint Mary's, where the sexton's wheel hung. I never saw a picture of Mary there, and her name sounded legendary and unreal, like St. George or King Arthur. My father would never have allowed us to be taken to a service, but it was permitted that we go inside while Grandma tidy the yellow chrysanthemums at the altar and Granddad clip the overgrown grass around the gravestones. I would wander around the nave, repelled by the bare, white cold, and Granddad would hide in the porch, cup his hands, and belt out in his deep bass voice a ghostly "Whhhoooooaaaaoooooo!" that made me jump out of my black patent shoes. I can still smell the grass, the dull flesh of chrysanthemums, the rain-smell of stone.

The fact that Grandma was, somehow, involved with God meant that she always had a vicar friend. When I was a child, it was Reverend Carr, the parish priest of that church. This vicar mattered to my grandmother in a way that I was very aware of.

Reverend Carr lived alone in the village rectory and was glad to be invited up to the house for tea in blue-and-white willow china by the fire. At the end of his visits, we children would line up to receive a coin from him, or boiled sweets. I don't remember a single word that came from his mouth—only a stooping, benign presence that somehow signified importance. Years later, Granddad told me that Rev. Carr had never married, though, as an Anglican vicar, he could have done so. He'd studied theology at Cambridge, and his prayers were careful and formal as the Sunday hymns whose overflowing chords and stolid beat filled me with such chilly dismay at school.

The vicar seemed lonely and careful, but I also remember the fact that he traveled to Italy, and, in that day and age, this gave him an air of exoticism.

I particularly remember the worried way we welcomed him one evening to tea when I was about eight. Some unspoken thing had happened. There were words about "You must be kind" and many whispered adult conversations in the kitchen. I was terrified that he might cry. To me, he seemed already the epitome of sadness: a man alone. We had recently gone, as a family, on an outing to the beach and eaten fish and chips in a restaurant. Across the room sat a bearded man eating a pile of shellfish alone. Stricken, I had grabbed my mother's hand and whispered for her to look. "He's having a lovely time!" she assured me. I didn't believe her for a second. As far as I was concerned, no solitary male could be happy.

The vicar may not have cried that afternoon, but the quietness of his voice (through which I could hear the creak of his leather shoes as he leaned forward to take a sandwich) was enough for me. I worked hard to be good and to laugh brightly at everything. But when he left, my throat swelled and my voice was jagged.

"Oh, it's nothing," soothed my grandmother by the fire once my brothers had run off. "He's having some trouble with the bishop, that's all. And men of the cloth have a lonely life . . ." Granddad stood at the door mock-playing an invisible violin to make me giggle.

"Granddad, *stop it!*" wailed Grandma.

But when I'd gone to bed in the cold back bedroom with a hot water bottle under my feet, I couldn't stop thinking of the lonely vicar across the field in the rectory. I found it almost un-bearable to imagine him alone in his large, empty house with the uncooked-in kitchen. Of course, I had no idea about prayer and its consolations, or otherwise. Living in a house with my parents and two brothers, it was inconceivable to me that a man could spend an evening on his own. My chest tightened again to tears.

Somehow, I imagined that the vicar's heart was broken. I knew from books that vicars were meant to have convivial houses and capable wives who baked cakes and counseled parishioners. The vicar's aloneness seemed to me, therefore, doubly cruel. His sadness seemed weighed by his reserve, his bookish and spare conversation. He didn't really know how to laugh at Granddad.

I lay in the crisp sheets and heard an owl's cry ribboning the night across the East Anglian fields and imagined that he would be hearing it too. It seemed to be searching, calling. The sound had the loneliness of Christ himself, stretched out eternally on a crucifix, hidden away on Grandma's bedroom wall.

The vicar, Grandma told me when I was ten, took to visiting Walsingham on his holidays. *Walsingham*, she would say, with great sing-song significance, as though it were a land of fantasy and laden with things I'd love to see.

"The church is dark inside," she whispered to me one afternoon by the snapping coal fire, "and smells like almonds—but Chinesey, you know, like the shop in Norwich? . . . It's full of gold and strange paintings and hundreds of candles, and messages written on pieces of paper all up and down the walls . . . like Christmas, really. I don't know, Moses." (She called me Moses— it took me decades to understand that she meant as a baby in the basket and not as a bearded prophet.) "Saint Mary's is too cold, the vicar says. Shall I put more flowers in, do you think? Something exotic? Lilies are ever so film-starish."

"Put in what you like," said Granddad. "Flowers and prayers don't keep you warm at night, do they gal?" And he tickled me and chased me down the hall.

We run to the odor of thy ointments

It was a summer weekend, and we were playing in the garden. Grandma was sitting at her easel painting anemones but not getting very far as she kept having to get up to get us ice cream or to stick a Band-Aid on a brother's knee. She had brought home new brushes from Reverend Carr and also a painting that he'd just finished, a copy of a Renaissance master that he wanted her to have. (For many years, I wondered if my grandmother were the true object of Rev. Carr's affections, but I think he was just grateful for her care.) I can hear her voice on that hot day, asking me to come in out of the sunshine to see where she should hang it.

In the lightness and weight of near sleep, I watch that painting on our lit stairwell, just as I watched it as a child in my grandparents' house (the oval entrance of the face in the dark hedge), and I dream the vicar's hand mirroring Raphael's, like two dancers in sync. Something must have been bewitched, magnetized, in the swimming alertness of the vicar's brain to achieve this art; his hand must have obeyed his eyes as seamlessly as a shadow to a man walking in early afternoon. This is how Mary watches God, I was beginning to see—for all of her choices are congruent with his will, meaning they are smooth hair through which a comb passes seamlessly, they are fine flour that flies through a sieve. Her thoughts and desires go with him like a girl who is running urgently down a street to meet her lover, and has the headwind behind her and with her. Her feet barely touch the ground. What tenderness I read in this depiction of her face. There were no owls in the Italian town where I lay sleepless, but I seemed to hear the silent imagined grief of the vicar again during those nights—the searching and the calling. And his painstaking time spent on Mary's face seemed, inexplicably, an answer.

The vicar gave the newly finished Raphael painting to my grandmother as a thank you, I would guess, for her kindness in whatever loneliness he found himself in. When he died, it was joined by the print of Lippi's painting of Lucrezia Buti that he had brought back from Florence and that would end up in the suitcase under my bed in London. There were other pictures on his back bedroom wall: a print of Leonardo's cave-dwelling *Madonna of the Rocks* and postcards from his trips to Italy and Walsingham: Bellini, Raphael, Fra Angelico. The vicar's back room was full of Mary's face, and when, one day, my grandmother walked in to clean, she gasped at this silent, hovering display, came out quickly, and shut the door. The vicar laughed. Sometimes in the evenings he went into the chilly room with an electric stove, drew the curtains, lighted a lamp, and sat to pray, he told her.

We run to the odor of thy ointments

My grandmother stored up that phrase; she loved the ring of it. People had been doing this, or something like this, for hundreds of years, the Reverend Carr told her, rocking on his feet.

There was something inexplicable about Walsingham, about the Rosary (from which the bishop had warned him off when he stopped by and saw a string of beads on the coffin stool). But the English used to know all about Mary. Even the English. Even before *Englaland* knew itself as England. When boar roamed the countryside and the language was guttural and strange. Even when that kingdom of disparate earldoms was forming.

There was nothing my grandmother loved more than a good story.

ᛢᛒ

Edith of Walsingham was born into worry, her nurse liked saying, in a time of signs, in the coming of the end of the world. The new millennium had passed, but as it approached, the year 1033, a thousand years since the death of Christ, spoke to the scalp and the back of the neck all over again. Edith was cradled on a step where the setting sun was large and untouched before it was swallowed by the level line of horizon. She was brought up with a sense of anxious mourning for this sun every evening and with the fear that it may not rise again. When a horse went lame, when another of her brothers and sisters died, when crops were killed off by late frost, when snow fell so high it covered windows, when the sun darkened at noon, when milk turned in hours and rats ambled across the kitchen floor, when meat spoiled, when diarrhea ran rampant, when ghosts were seen patrolling fields, when outlaws were sighted, when battles were lost, the grown-ups exchanged looks, they fastened the storehouses, they stopped speaking; they prayed. Edith's bedtime stories were filled with lamps, virgins, and thieves. He would come in the dead of night; they would not know the hour. Two women would be working in the field: one would be swept off and saved, the other *not*. From the age of five, Edith slept with her crucifix in one hand and her knife in the other.

"It's that time," her nurse taught her from before she could talk. "There won't be many more days."

Light was squeezed to a few hours. Her cold toes became waxy and white. Men, her own brothers, would march from the house and never return.

Sub tuum praesidium confugimus, sancta dei genitrix

And yet the days always did return. The children who were not buried, grew. The brothers who did come back had children. Edith's home was warmed by large hearth fires, and her plate was always full. Childbirth didn't kill her. She owned jewelry and heavy clothes, and she loved, sometimes, the sense of everything being a world away. She was in an ocean of flat land: in summer, the grasses rippled like the sea a few miles away. She was pale and blue-eyed and her hair never darkened beyond the color of wheat. Rich and fair, they called her *Richeldis*.

It was the beginning of winter. Her eldest had been striding back and forth talking battle, like his father. His father, who was rarely there, had been doing that same thing this past week: striding back and forth for warmth but also to show off and talk up his latest schemes to a crowd of drunk listeners. Edith watched her son. He was more slender than his father, still not fully fleshed. She could not imagine him bearing the armor and marching away. She could almost still lift him up in her arms— at least, she could remember the time that she could. That night, as he marched and the other children shrieked and baited him, she saw some tinge on his cheeks and a shininess in his eyes that sent distant alarums ringing in her mind. She was still laughing when the alarum's message reached her mouth and eyes: fever. She shouted his name through the din, but no one heard. They were shouting for him to go outside for a game; someone had run to fetch sticks, and there were more down by the barn. She saw that her son's eyes did not hear. His face switched white. But the children were pushing him, and his feet tottered out into the night snow with a procession caterwauling around him—and he fell like a hurled rock onto the ice. The children fanned into a circle, like water receiving that stone, and the ice took the moment, the white boy on the ground with vomit trickling from his mouth, and held it.

She had seen death before—in cows, in children, and in both her parents—and she thought she saw it now: the empty-room vacancy of his eyes and the mouth slack like the freshly hanged. His still girlish jawbone seemed to grow before her eyes. In this ruined face, she would swear later, her son was not there.

But a woman servant—not waiting for Edith to find her voice—searched frantically for the beat in his neck and found it, and two men carried him up to his bed where he would stay for months too weak to do more than wet his sheets and shiver. Edith didn't leave him through all of that time. She checked the fire and called for more broth; she wiped his brow and wrists with a cold cloth. With some irony, she reflected that she had not expected *this*. Lately, her mind had run ahead to when this boy and his brothers would join the armies of men for their bouts of killing and quelling. But not this loss; she had not thought about this loss; not now.

The prospect of losing her son opened a door she made a point of keeping shut. She could not live with the constant thought of her husband's death in battle or the loss of a child to diphtheria or diarrhea. But now that this child receded from her too quickly for hope, all panic assailed her through the open door of possibility. The end of the world, she wanted to say to her nurse (long dead), is happening.

But then, the end of the world happens every day, to count-less people. As she sat beside her son's bedside, she closed her eyes and couldn't help but see the body of her brother lanced, one eye hanging out on his cheek. She saw her nephew decapitated, the eyes blinking for long seconds as the head rumbled away. She wished she didn't know these things, but people talked. People had to unburden. And at least, knowing, she could pray into the darkness as she heard the owls cry. For if a man dies and no one prays, it is as if he never existed, the old priest used to say. She knew he was wrong, yet felt he was right. Our suffering wrestles into form and sense not only in God, but in God in the hearts and prayers of others.

A crucifix was nailed above her son's bed, and she prayed gazing on it as her son's breaths came faster and shorter. The wooden Christ on the cross was slack and abandoned in his suf-fering. "My God, my God, why have you forsaken me?" It was this line of all of Scripture that tore most at her throat: the Christ was abandoned by the whole of humanity. Even his Mother would have looked very small from where he was, at the height of his agony. No one could be with him in this elevated aloneness. He seemed to rise on the steepest hill—unable to touch his Fa-ther above, betrayed or deserted by his friends below.

The abandonment at the supreme moment of the crucifixion, what an abyss of love on both sides!

The call of the forsaken God, Creator of everything, who took on the awful abandonment even of himself, even of his peo-ple, struck Edith in the vein of her self-pity. She couldn't reach her son, who was too far gone in illness and creeping further from her minute by minute. She couldn't reach her God (she was too far gone in misery). It was a terrible comparison to make, she knew. But those words of Jesus on the cross repeated in her ears with the cries of the owls across the flat East Anglian land.

(At night, when owls cry, there never seems to be an answer. To the vicar's loneliness, there seemed to be no answer, to Marianne in her white room, and to Mischa as he wept beside his sleeping partner. There seems to be no answer, and God knows this. He calls too, and there is no adequate response from the mass of humanity.)

Edith had an army of women to help her with the washing and feeding of her young man. He seemed already gone. The spark, the character, the tone of voice—how quickly these things were snuffed, leaving—what? The soul? No soul could be so faceless, surely, so dead. Even a whisper was too much for him, his breathing hoarse and hot and his eyes full of slippery visions. He had been with her for fifteen years, and she thought if he left now she wouldn't want to stay in the world. The thought would have shamed her, if there had been room in her heart for shame. She had a husband, other children, money, God. It was the thought of one more death—especially this death—that tipped the scales in her heart. As though the sun wouldn't have the muscle to rise anymore.

She prayed at his bedside and had the cook boil broth by the gallon. She couldn't pray by the book. She could only utter and exclaim. But through those hurled prayers, through broth and time, the light in his face changed, became workaday. Became like the fields when the mist has risen. One morning, he whispered her name.

In a matter of days, a fieldhand was called in from the barn to help him stand—the sores at the back of him were livid and shiny as pig grease—and he collapsed back onto the bed. But a week later, he walked as far as the hearth—great lurching, trembling steps. The day after that, he ate a handful of bread.

The spring came, muddy and cold. Gold and purple crocuses sprang up in the wood where Edith walked after breakfast, and daffodils filled the gardens. He was back with her; she had not lost him. The relief made her physically bend over to the ground every few steps. One day she supposed he'd march off with his father and she would be left in that desert of wondering, her only hope that they would return with someone else's blood dried in the folds of their necks and the creases of their hands. Edith could not know that her own *Pietà* awaited her—not of herself and her child, but herself and her husband. (There will even be a statue of Edith finding Harold on a battlefield. The sculptor will avoid the awkward facts: that his head was cut off, a leg torn from him, his torso disemboweled, and his chest pierced. The sculpture will show, instead, Edith's arms around his neck as though trying to pull the man back into life.) But Edith knew, even then as she made that grateful springtime walk, that the world was ending. She knew everything about history and possibility. Even so, in that moment, she had this: her son saved and with her. Gratitude, the old priest would say, brings a soul closer to God.

The wind never stopped running; it bashed every wall and bone. She prayed. She visited the sick and took herbs and tinctures; she visited the poor and took bread and cast-off cloaks and mittens. She visited the chapel and prayed and prayed, many *Paters* and *Sub tuum praesidiums*. Every visit was long as she carefully prayed for all the dead: the babies, the soldiers, the parents, aunts, uncles, earls, freemen, nursemaids, and farmers. The wind rattled the window and made the chaplain cough; her own feet turned numb. She prayed as though words could erode this terrible sense of an ending that she was born into, strengthen her son's legs, cleanse the dead blood from her husband's beard, protect the men on the return march that was always thinner, every time. But most of all—almost as an afterthought, except it was this that kept her there in that cold chapel—she was newly thankful.

"Min dryhten God Aelmihtig, min dryhten God Aelmihtig, min dryhten God Aelmihtig." She says this as she wakes, before she's put a foot out of bed into the freezing air. She can hear the sound of logs snapping and spitting as the fire gets going. She pulls a rug around her shoulders, slides to kneel beside the bed and crosses herself:

Domine, labia mea aperies

As she finishes her prayers, she listens, but there's no noise other than the usual tramp of footsteps, pans bashing, men and women complaining of the cold. Children are running through the fields wiping whiteness off the grass with their boots and screaming about some game.

"Put your hats on!" she yells, but no one answers.

They say that she spoke to Mary. Was it directly, or by rote? Did she hear the words and listen hard, or were she and Edith talking for years about the ending of this life and the remarkable relief of the next? Edith's psalter is illustrated with drawings made by monks. The Psalms are in her own language as well as Latin, and she has written next to a picture of Mary her favorite prayers and the names of her children in a list.

She knows her God through the rising of the sun; she knows her Lord by the sacrifice of the Mass and the staunching of her hunger on his flesh; she knows the Ghost by the carrying of the day, the arrival of bread on the plate, and news by messenger that her husband is safe again.

What happened with Mary?

One night, in early spring, Edith kneels at her bedside and asks for ways to thank the Virgin.

"This is our world and it's safe," she would tell her children when they were frightened. "Look at the starlings in the hedges, and the rowan berries on the trees. Look at the sheep in the fields and listen for the sea far away. You can't hear it? Good. Because we are in our own little kingdom and nothing bad is going to happen. We are surrounded by fields upon fields and under the shelter of Our Lady's mantle. She is watching over us."

That night she kneels at her bedside and gives thanks for the umpteenth time, but this time asking what she can *do* to honor the Virgin. And Mary comes to her. As she would come to the shepherd children in a field, as she would come to the Mexican peasant, to the poor girl by the rubbish dump, and the French nun, and so many others, it's almost impossible to tell what is Mary and what is lies and stories; what are visions and what are dreams; what is the entrance of a real person into a room and where the grain of God is genuine.

Mary comes to Edith and shows her the house of the Annunciation.

(I can't escape that moment. Not even in a gallery in London, with God, to so many, an incongruous idea, dwarfed by the confusion of traffic and lights outside. In the gallery: the bent heads, the lilies, the holy moment as tourists line up their phones or ask the way to the bathroom. In an almost deserted convent in Rome, Mary is there in a chapel without her angel but with lilies keeping vigil as she hears the news. In a side street behind a black grille, a flaky image of Mary with the angel and a bouquet of flowers thrust into the mesh. In churches, on walls, in giftshops, on postcards, we are witness to that moment. It is the happening that we all look for. In bottles of whiskey and Mescaline trips, in books and the architecture of music, on dancefloors, in racing cars, up mountains and by water, we are looking for that moment of pact. We hear God calling for it too, in the cry of the owl, in our own unanswered misery, in the *scirocco* wind in an empty house. We hear it in the cry of Jesus on the cross and the anguish of the bereaved. We long for the consolation of God's lips on ours—his cry met by ours. And while the churched can meet God in church, the vast unchurched, the seekers, the discouraged, the far-away will often look for Mary without knowing it. Mary: searcher, lady of the lost, God's outlier.)

As Edith bends in prayer and covers her face with her hands, Mary comes to her. She comes, I think, because Edith calls on her day and night. Edith's whole life has been patterned with greeting Mary, from the first *Ave* and Psalm at sunrise to the Magnificat at sundown to the last *Ave* before she sleeps. She is doing with her words what the Old Believers did when they greeted a priest: she is touching earth and pointing to heaven, touching earth and pointing to heaven, touching earth and pointing to heaven. Mary is the place where heaven and earth meet.

Edith is on her knees, but she sees Mary, and most of all hears her, and she is drenched in her voice and face. There is such rightness in them that it's beyond anything describable, beyond anything anyone could paint. If an artist had taken a geometer's instruments and crafted, as Fra Lippi tried to, the perfect face, he would fall short of Mary's perfection. But it is not the anodyne perfection we find in perfect noses and shaped eyebrows. It's the breath-stopping, rosy light-on-a-puddle, momentary beauty that Fra Lippi struggled for. Her voice is musical—not lyrical and sliding in song but so harmonious that it fills Edith with love in every part of her mind and body.

Three times Mary shows her the house in Nazareth where the angel came to her. It's a place white with heat and purple flowers that Edith has never seen before. She has never felt so safe. Every wall of this place is touched with an abundance she can't identify or describe. Mary shows her the measurements, the length of the walls, the height, and Edith takes them into herself. Mary tells her she should build the same house in those empty flat fields where the bloodied men return, and "all that seek me there shall find succor." There is no more pain in Edith's bones, as if this voice were medicine. She falls asleep with the sight of Mary in her eyes, and as soon as she wakes, before the servants are out, and the children can run wild, she speeds outside to a glistening spring morning. The cobwebs and grass are alive with dew—but two rectangular areas, the size of small houses, lie dry as a bone.

They said it was like Gideon's fleece, laid out overnight, and Edith had to choose which dry patch of land to build on. But having chosen one and instructed a hastily assembled group of men, they couldn't make the thing work. The measurements were all wrong, the foreman said; it wouldn't take shape. Edith was used to workmen saying this (who isn't?) and gave them more hours of tutting and shaking their heads. But they could not get beyond marking out the foundations.

So neither the one who plants nor the one who waters is anything, but only God who gives the growth

In every crop, every poem, every banquet, in every painting of Mary, we can only fudge with instruments and measurements. Without the holy breath, the artifact does not live.

"Unless the Lord builds the house, those who build it labor in vain," Edith reads at sundown, and stays on her knees as many hours as she can, rereading those words, and praying through the night. "You are God's field, God's building," she finds herself repeating. She wakes as light crawls through the curtains and, legend has it, goes outside to find the house completed on the *other* spot. Mary built it in the darkness as she prayed.

I am the field that bore in season
wheat for the sacred mysteries

No one speaks of the hidden time. Before dawn, I imagine that Edith stood in the penetrating cold, looking at the small wooden house, and knowing Mary. Perhaps Edith and Mary danced for joy. No one was awake. In the moonless black, the birds hadn't started to sing. The stars waxed. She thought she could hear the sea. And God had never seemed closer. Mary, Daughter of the Father, Mother of the Son, Bride of the Spirit, was with her. In the hidden hours before exclamation and the young tramping in and out of this new wooden house, before the youngest could ask for it as his castle and the girl want it for her sheep, before the men with their hammers and tools could roll up and suck their teeth and push and pull the joints, the way that workmen do, there was this: a wildcard of creation that seemed destined for nothing and no one but Edith in that moment.

But they will come, Mary must have told her. They will come.

Before that, there are more hidden hours, and then days and weeks. Then some make the journey on foot from Norwich, and crowds will roll up—from London, Scotland, France, beyond— but Edith will not be there to see it. Those early days, the house of the Annunciation is all hers. The place of this happening that reveals most fully to us that we are made in his image and likeness. The place that explains Mary as a tower, a mirror, a telegraph wire, a pair of hands, a bringer, a woman of the thin place.

iv

Woman clothed with the sun, with the moon under her feet,
and on her head a crown of twelve stars

After our hours deploring the patriarchal Church, it was my
New Yorker friend Maisie I'd been most abashed to tell the news
of my conversion. When I climbed her stairs one day and con-
fessed, before I had even taken my coat off, that I was Catholic, I
had to add, "It must seem odd to you."

She looked annoyed. "Why? Why would I be surprised? You
found your soul; you didn't lose your mind."

Over the decade that followed, Maisie stayed unwavering in
her respect, and even curiosity, about my faith. As I stepped into
her house in the middle of a pandemic, she showed me a blue
icon of Mary in her hallway and told me that her ex painted it
years ago and she'd decided to hang it up.

Maisie's house was vast and dark and strangely full of images
of Mary and Jesus—Byzantine icons, deeply grained wooden
sculptures, figurines from South America and Africa. For someone who was not religious ("My mother was Catholic, my father
was Jewish, so they canceled each other out"), Maisie had a lot of
religious art. But also Japanese silks, Ukrainian paintings, African pottery, and Brazilian folk art. As she arthritically climbed
the spiral iron staircase to her roof garden, she craned her red-
head backward to say she had a lot to tell me; she was glad I'd
come. She was in a lot of pain. And, like so many of us at that
time, lonely. We had taken to swapping book recommendations

among her pots of cactus and olive trees on her terrace, and sharing drams of whiskey from a flask when it was cold.

We talked for half an hour up there on the roof. The wind was icy and bothersome, and I was beginning to shiver in my coat, but Maisie began a long story involving her parents in New Jersey and a wealthy aunt. I was skim-listening. I could hear the bells for Mass and wondered if I should make my excuses and go, but realized that both Maisie and I relied on these chats for our sanity, and while I had the Mass to make me feel better now that the churches were open, she still didn't have anywhere to go. Maisie's story went on. I had just finished Donna Tartt's *The Goldfinch* and had been telling her about the central painting and how it shone, how it represented beauty and hope through a dark narrative. Maisie was telling me about finding a rolled-up piece of linoleum in an attic after an aunt died. I looked at the time out of the corner of an eye and shifted to the edge of my chair.

"It was filthy, and kinda cracked. I was scared to unroll it, but I didn't know what it was. I guessed it was a piece of floor covering, you know? So I gently flattened it out on a table, and I could see it was some kind of a picture. But filthy. I thought I'd better trash it along with a bunch of other stuff. Gimme some more of that."

I poured a fingerful more whiskey into her plastic cup.

"Anyways, around that time I was working in an office and there was this young intern, and I was telling him about what I found. Right away he says, 'I know a guy who's an art restorer, if you want him to take a look at that picture.' Well I kinda did and I didn't, if you know what I mean. I highly doubted it was anything much. But one day I called up this guy's friend and took the rolled up linoleum to a place on the Upper East Side where this person had an antique store. The restorer took a look at the filthy thing on his table, and he tells me he'd like to work on it. I say 'How much?' and he says two thousand bucks. He must have seen my expression because then he says, 'Look, I really would like to do this, and you can give me eight hundred for my time.' I couldn't believe it. I said okay, you know? Well, about a couple of months later I get a call saying I should go down to the antique store. As I walked the street toward the shop, from yards away I could see that the window was lit up and there was this incredible painting right in the center, the main thing, you know?" She presses her fingers to her lips and gulps. "Honestly, Sally, you wouldn't believe it. It was my picture. Wait, I wanna show you."

I followed her back down the iron staircase and into the hallway of the house. She rooted around in a drawer and pulled out a file full of documents. I saw a letter from the National Gallery in London and another from a US art dealer. She handed me a photo: it was of a painting of Mary, of course, with St. Joseph and St. Catherine of Alexandria—but Mary was the focus, she was the light at its center, she and her child. St. Catherine, kneeling on the broken wheel of her torture, was being united in mystical marriage to Jesus, and it was Mary who was uniting them. And again, as I studied that painting, I understood the importance of her hands.

"I loved that," Maisie was saying, "I loved this smart woman Catherine for standing up to torture in order to have a life of the mind."

The colors in the painting were cream, brown, and delicate ocher. Mary's face was untroubled as water. The composition had movement as if everything else was in flux around Mary. Mary and her child were the anchor at the center.

"I just stood there in that freezing street and cried," Maisie said. "I couldn't believe it. I couldn't believe the beauty."

The painting was by a sixteenth-century North Italian master and was locked up in art storage in New York now, like the painting in *The Goldfinch*.

I found myself crying too. It was such a serving of unexpected beauty in the midst of loneliness, cold wind, and cheap Irish whiskey.

ॐ

Eventually, I got to visit England.

I traveled to the lanes and fields that the vicar and Edith walked in East Anglia. The village wasn't easy to reach: a bus from Norwich and a taxi from the nearest village, or another infrequent bus. The lanes were winding. As I looked out at the fields and stiles, I thought of my grandparents. Those were the horizons of my childhood: muddy walks and bicycle rides, the nights listening to the owls.

Well into his eighties, Granddad, alone by then and with his slicked hair standing up in tufts, would stand in his back garden and sweep the vast sky with his hand once again: "Who'd want to go anywhere else?" Here was better: flat fields and a flutter of birds at the feeder, a ginger cat and a hedgehog that appeared at nine every evening to be fed. Of course, Granddad was dead now too. The vicar's oil painting was on my stairs in Italy, and a photo of Granddad with the ginger cat hung in my kitchen.

North Norfolk, East Anglia, the place the vicar spent his holiday weekends, felt like home. This is Mary's place in my country. She appeared there, when the Kingdom of England was creaky and new and the Norman conquest was yet to happen. She came to a place of desolate fields with grey skies, to a country that was barely a country at all.

These days, Walsingham is a quaint collection of Tudor houses, churches, ruins, and shops selling icons and statues. A place of silent confusion and mystery. History has garbled what happened there and where it happened, and even to whom Mary appeared and in what manner. But some things are extant and unarguable, like the vertiginous stone arch of an ancient priory that stands in a green garden long after all the building that it heralded fell down, was torched, looted, and desecrated.

Walsingham is a place where groups of pilgrims show up and stare, avidly, at nothing.

I haven't been to Lourdes, Fatima, Knock, or any other of the numerous apparition sites, but I do know that if you go to those places, you find a point of happening: the grotto at Lourdes, the sheltered spot at Cova da Iria, the wall of a parish church in damp Irish countryside. In Walsingham, there is no easy-to-find sign; what happened here was beaten down like a field of crops by King Henry's reformers. And, as new buildings eventually sprang up to commemorate it, the shrines and churches seemed somewhat awkwardly placed, like the healing of an imprecisely set bone. I unpacked my suitcase in a Tudor-beamed bedroom and put my newest Marian image, Our Lady of Perpetual Help, on the nightstand. I'd come to like icons; they didn't try to *be* Mary but just gave me a window to look through as I prayed.

My oldest friend, Mel, peered at a medieval stone entrance across the street.

"We need a guidebook," she said for the second time, falling into an armchair. The story was simple enough, but knowing where things were or where they happened was tricky.

I felt responsible for the trip and, strangely enough, for Mary. Mel was once a happy Protestant who was taught to distrust what she calls "the whole Mary thing." After so many years, I felt a calling to defend what I still couldn't entirely understand.

Where Mary appeared to Edith (or "Richeldis" as she has become more commonly known), no one could really say. Whether it was in a field, or beside her bed, or somewhere else in her manor house (long gone).

Through the stone entrance across the street, among those green slopes and snowdrops in spring, there was a sign by the tall ruined arch that told us that this was where the first house of the Annunciation was built that night as Edith prayed. The large Protestant manor nearby was well-kept and silent. Up a damp lane, the Orthodox church was an old converted railway station. The new Catholic church was in the middle of the village. The main shrine (which locals call "the barn" because of its austere architecture) was out of the village because that's where pilgrims used to walk from, and that's where we would find the old "Slipper Chapel" where they used to remove their shoes to walk the last mile to the house of the Annunciation barefoot. There was another set of ancient ruins. Of what, of when? Again, Mel suggested a guidebook. We began to think about dinner. And wine.

I thought I understood the terrain. Twenty-nine and fresh from the Plains, I wandered in bewilderment around Walsingham when I was taken there by my mother, who knew my inexplicable fascination for Mary. As an atheist, I could find her nowhere. I remember driving down tiny lanes with a map and getting out at churches, wondering what they meant. I came back the year I was forty-nine, enraptured with Mary in Scripture, as a Catholic and fellow mother. I walked the fields that Edith walked and thought I came closer to solving the mystery.

But it was on this trip I would come nearest to finding her.

I was trying to explain to Mel where everything was, where it happened. "It" lifted on the breeze and flew. That evening, we set off randomly. There were no cars in the village; we dawdled in the road. We looked at the rosaries and honey in shops. We loved peering inside windows; even the houses were full of statues. The most ubiquitous of all the images was Our Lady of Walsingham in painted ceramic or stone. This 1922 statue was based on the image of the medieval seal of Walsingham Priory. It shows a stately Mary with a Saxon crown seated on the throne of Wisdom, a playful toddler on her left knee. In her right hand she holds a lily, symbol of purity, and under her feet is the toad-stone—East Anglian symbol of evil. On my phone, I showed Mel a photograph of a thirteenth-century statue reported to be the original Lady of Walsingham, the one that was supposedly burned in 1539 when the shrine was destroyed on the orders of Henry VIII. Some say that this Madonna was actually saved by the Vicar of Langham, who handed it to the recusant own-ers of Langham Hall for safekeeping. This "Lady of Langham" is ravaged: her blossoming stem is lost, her crown is gone. Her baby's head has disappeared. But there is still likeness enough to make me believe that the Langham statue was the first Lady of Walsingham statue. In both pieces, the full length of Mary's strong legs is clearly visible beneath her gown. In both, the Holy Child sits on the left leg and reaches protectively across his mother's chest, his fingers and thumb outstretched. In the older piece, Mary's eyes are gone. But the queenly power of her posture remains.

Mel and I each bought a soapstone replica of the new Lady, with her eyes, her crown, her flowers, and her baby restored.

As we walked, we couldn't stop laughing; it was relief. We hadn't seen each other for two years, and we'd been housebound for months. But we always laughed. At school, we giggled so much we had to be separated. Even now, both fifty-year-old con-verts, we had to sit apart in chapel. We could be in any situation, telepathically see the comedy in a detail, and weep with ago-nizing mirth. Mel was the softest, kindest soul I knew. Subject to vivid dreams, her unconscious often rose up in conversation, making her give tongue to prophecy or nonsense. Wherever in the world I lived, we called each other every week and arranged to meet to discuss the whys and wherefores of our lives. She'd known me almost my whole life and deeper than almost any-one else. After dinner, we sat outside the old village pub and drank red wine and laughed so hard that people turned and smiled at us.

As usual, there was much to discuss. My uncle was unwell. His now shrunken sphere of socializing, coupled with my irresolvable distances, meant that I couldn't see him as much as I wanted and needed to. We had inched through literature and reasoning to find our bond was, after all, untouched by my conversion. I wanted, now, to be near him and the rest of my family. But would Fabio live for long stretches in England once he had retired? He *said* he would, but could he be happy under this grey sky?

There are many lands, and Mary meets us in all of them—but she always whispers our own language in our ear. Fabio called every evening of my trip. We changed and formed and fused together, like the pile of rusty chains that my old boyfriend photographed by the Thames. Every evening, Fabio told me what he was cooking—those island parcels of pasta filled with *pecorino* and potato or roasted pork and fennel; the wines and the oil—hoping to make me miss home. But I did miss it. This missing didn't go away in any country in which I found myself. I was already seeing that the Lady I should turn to, the one we all turn to ultimately, is Our Lady of Exile. The Woman who knows that we, in our particular state, can only be known fully by God. That we will only ever be complete with him. The Lady who, in the meantime, wants us to accept her as our home.

We walked the holy mile out of the village just as the sun was setting. The walls of the ruined Franciscan monastery glowed in old-gold light. The sky fell like ruched grey silk. It was unbearably beautiful. The fields were endless. Here Edith walked, and here Mary walks.

Next morning, we finally found the large Anglican shrine that Reverend Carr visited and that my grandmother spoke about so long ago. There were lots of large Indian families walking the gardens and groups of pilgrims. Children were playing around the stations of the cross and elderly rested on benches. Some were Catholic, but some were Hindu. Hindus, I had discovered, revere Mary as a miracle worker.

Inside the church, there was the darkness that Grandma described, and the almond smell, the pieces of paper tacked up and down the walls, the yellow and red paintings, the icons, the altars where the vicar liked to linger. We stepped into a room within a room and were met with gold and the heat of many banks of candles. Here she was as Queen, cradling a long-stemmed golden lily and, on her other knee, the Christ child. It was as if they couldn't make her more splendid. They exhausted every theatrical device: a gold shell, larger than her image, sat atop her heavy crown; her veil of lace and gold-fringed green splayed out beneath her like the sea beneath a tiny boat.

And there, before mother and child, was the grown Christ crucified in silver.

Silence, say the statues, and the thousands of women dressed like her—the flat-cracked faces by Barnaba da Modena, the wooden expressions of Giotto, the empty-window eyes of Cimabue. They are only with us to remind us of that fire that can never be replicated on this earth: the touch of God to one woman. *La soberana doctora de la escuelas divinas*: in Mary's littleness (it can only be in littleness), she drinks the wisdom of God. Ruth was a link in the chain that brought Jesus to us. Esther and Judith were women saviors in their own small (yet mighty) ways. All spoke of Mary, as the grasses speak of the wind, which speaks of God. Small woman of the hospital wards, the galleries, the deserts and the coffeeshops, the processions and the backyard, you come to us in silence; you disappear in searching.

But look upon the lovely face whose brightness most
resembles Love, since that radiance alone
can prepare you for the light and presence of the Son

In this room—a copy of that room that Mary built for Edith, which was a copy of her room in Nazareth—the Virgin conceived God himself. I always imagined her outside at the Annunciation, in a courtyard. Or a field. But it hardly matters. The air is dense with prayer. It is light caught in a jar. I have walked into a room where a woman is seated and waiting.

"And from that hour the disciple took her into his own home." But the Greek text speaks not so much of a house that we ask her into: ἴδια means *inner being*. John took her into *himself*.

It comes to me as I stand in prayer: the call has been answered. For while God swells with contentment at the response of any one of us, your answer, Mary, your yes, is the cry that he was waiting for from the beginning of all time. In all of creation, I realize now, there is no one like you. No one can answer his desperate calls the way that you do, daughter of Zion. The Son answers the Father as he hangs in his agony. But God is still crying. In the dark fields, in cities, Father, Son, and Spirit call for an answer from humanity. As a child, when I listened to the owl's cry at night, when I felt the loneliness of the vicar like the loneliness of the man-God stretched out in his Passion, I was listening, without knowing it, for your answering cry, the essential link between man and God. There is no purer response than yours. It is a song that allows all of us to sing.

I wait for the two pilgrims who are praying beside me to leave, and Mel to tell me she is going off to take photos, and I fall to my knees.

HOLY MOTHER OF GOD • HOLY VIRGIN OF VIRGINS • MOTHER OF CHRIST

MOTHER OF THE CHURCH • MOTHER OF MERCY

MOTHER OF DIVINE GRACE • MOTHER OF HOPE • MOTHER MOST PURE

MOTHER MOST CHASTE • MOTHER INVIOLATE • MOTHER UNDEFILED

MOTHER MOST AMIABLE • MOTHER MOST ADMIRABLE

MOTHER OF GOOD COUNSEL • MOTHER OF OUR CREATOR

MOTHER OF OUR SAVIOR • VIRGIN MOST PRUDENT

VIRGIN MOST VENERABLE • VIRGIN MOST RENOWNED

VIRGIN MOST POWERFUL • VIRGIN MOST MERCIFUL

VIRGIN MOST FAITHFUL • MIRROR OF JUSTICE • SEAT OF WISDOM

CAUSE OF OUR JOY • SPIRITUAL VESSEL • VESSEL OF HONOR

SINGULAR VESSEL OF DEVOTION • MYSTICAL ROSE • TOWER OF DAVID

TOWER OF IVORY • HOUSE OF GOLD • ARK OF THE COVENANT

GATE OF HEAVEN • MORNING STAR • HEALTH OF THE SICK

REFUGE OF SINNERS • SOLACE OF MIGRANTS • COMFORT OF THE AFFLICTED

HELP OF CHRISTIANS • QUEEN OF ANGELS • QUEEN OF PATRIARCHS

QUEEN OF PROPHETS • QUEEN OF APOSTLES • QUEEN OF MARTYRS

QUEEN OF CONFESSORS • QUEEN OF VIRGINS • QUEEN OF ALL SAINTS

QUEEN CONCEIVED WITHOUT ORIGINAL SIN

QUEEN ASSUMED INTO HEAVEN • QUEEN OF THE MOST HOLY ROSARY

QUEEN OF FAMILIES • QUEEN OF PEACE • MOTHER OF THE CRUCIFIED

SORROWFUL MOTHER • MOURNFUL MOTHER • MOTHER SIGHING

MOTHER AFFLICTED • MOTHER FORSAKEN • MOTHER DESOLATE

MOTHER MOST SAD • MOTHER SET AROUND WITH ANGUISH

MOTHER OVERWHELMED BY GRIEF • MOTHER TRANSFIXED BY A SWORD

MOTHER CRUCIFIED IN THY HEART • MOTHER BEREAVED OF THY SON

SIGHING DOVE • MOTHER OF DOLORS • FOUNT OF TEARS

SEA OF BITTERNESS • FIELD OF TRIBULATION • MASS OF SUFFERING

MIRROR OF PATIENCE • ROCK OF CONSTANCY • REMEDY IN PERPLEXITY

JOY OF THE AFFLICTED • ARK OF THE DESOLATE

REFUGE OF THE ABANDONED • SHIELD OF THE OPPRESSED

CONQUEROR OF THE INCREDULOUS • SOLACE OF THE WRETCHED

MEDICINE OF THE SICK • HELP OF THE FAINT • STRENGTH OF THE WEAK

PROTECTRESS OF THOSE WHO FIGHT • HAVEN OF THE SHIPWRECKED

CALMER OF TEMPESTS • COMPANION OF THE SORROWFUL

RETREAT OF THOSE WHO GROAN • TERROR OF THE TREACHEROUS

STANDARD-BEARER OF THE MARTYRS • TREASURE OF THE FAITHFUL

LIGHT OF CONFESSORS • PEARL OF VIRGINS • COMFORT OF WIDOWS

JOY OF ALL SAINTS • QUEEN OF THY SERVANTS • DWELLING-PLACE OF GOD

TEMPLE OF THE HOLY GHOST • SUN NEVER SETTING

MOON NEVER WANING • MORNING-STAR

TABERNACLE OF GOD AMONG MEN • LILY AMONG THORNS

GATE OF HEAVEN • FLAWLESS MIRROR • GARDEN ENCLOSED

FOUNTAIN OF LIVING WATERS • PROMISED TO THE PATRIARCHS

FORETOLD BY THE PROPHETS • ENVISIONED BY THE UPRIGHT

CONSOLATION OF ADAM THROUGH THE CRUSHING OF THE INFERNAL SERPENT'S HEAD

IMMACULATE HEART • MATER DOLOROSA • CO-REDEMPTRIX

MEDIATRIX • ADVOCATE • SPOUSE OF THE HOLY SPIRIT

DAUGHTER OF THE FATHER • MOTHER OF THE SON

IMMACULATE CONCEPTION • FULL OF GRACE • ASSUMED INTO HEAVEN

STAR OF THE SEA • OUR LADY OF PERPETUAL SUCCOR

OUR LADY OF LOURDES • OUR LADY OF FATIMA • OUR LADY OF LA SALETTE

OUR LADY OF KIBEHO • OUR LADY OF GUADALUPE

OUR LADY OF WALSINGHAM • OUR LADY OF KNOCK

OUR LADY UNTIER OF KNOTS • CONTAINER OF THE UNCONTAINABLE

THEOTOKOS • LIVING TEMPLE OF GOD • INTERCESSOR

ARK OF THE FLOOD • MANNA • ROD OF AARON • FLEECE OF GIDEON

CITY OF GOD • NEW JERUSALEM • ROOT OF JESSE • KEY OF HEAVEN

SCRIPTURE'S COMMENT AND GLOSS • MEDICINE CHEST OF GOD

CELL OF THE WORD • ABYSS OF HONEY • CASKET OF CELESTIAL INCENSE

SAW OF DEATH • GRACIOUS VIRGIN • SHIELD OF SINNERS • NEW EVE

WOMAN CLOTHED WITH THE SUN, MOON, AND STARS • TERROR OF DEMONS

OUR LADY OF GOOD COUNSEL • OUR LADY OF REVELATION

OUR LADY OF GRACE • OUR LADY OF HOPE • OUR LADY OF JOY

OUR LADY OF LORETO • OUR LADY OF MOUNT CARMEL

OUR LADY OF NAZARETH • OUR LADY OF POMPEI • OUR LADY OF SORROWS

OUR LADY OF THE SNOWS • LAMP BY THE BEDSIDE • PANE OF GLASS

AIR WE BREATHE • WONDROUS ROBE • WILD WEB

WAY OUT OF THE GUTTER • SANITY IN CHAOS • ROAD TO GOD

ROOTED TREE • LUNGS OF PRAYER • SECRET LISTENER • VIGIL-KEEPER

Notes

EPIGRAPHS

viii **"Wild air, world-mothering air"**: From "The Blessed Virgin compared to the Air we Breathe" by Gerard Manley Hopkins.

viii **"I love all things that need my lover's life"**: From "The Blessed Virgin Mary Compared to a Window" by Thomas Merton.

viii **"Tell all the Truth but tell it slant"**: Poem 1129 by Emily Dickinson.

PRELUDE: MY FIRST MARYS

4 **sitting at the gate:** Wisdom 6:14. The identification of Mary with Wisdom, and the Bride in the Song of Solomon, has become obfuscated with time. These strong identifications are reflected in the antiphons of the medieval *Little Office of the Blessed Virgin Mary* and the preconciliar Roman Breviary and lectionary, and the dynamic of the relationship of Mary to Wisdom is explained luminously by Joseph Ratzinger (Pope Benedict XVI) in his *Daughter Zion: Meditations on the Church's Marian Belief*, trans. John M. McDermott (San Francisco: Ignatius, 1985), 26.

7 *de Maria numquam satis*: "Of Mary, never enough" (St. Bernard of Clairvaux).

CHAPTER ONE: NEW EVE

13 **"She is more beautiful than the sun"**: Wisdom 7:29–30.

16 **"She hastens to make herself known to those who desire her"**: Wisdom 6:13.

22 **Paolo and Francesca:** Paolo and Francesca are lovers condemned to be together forever, buffeted by gales in canto 5 of Dante's *Inferno*.

24 **"thinking with the blood":** See Martin Amis, *Experience* (New York: Vintage, 2000), 260.

28 **"such a smile within her eyes":** Dante Alighieri, *Paradiso*, canto 15, from Ned Denny, *B (After Dante)* (Manchester: Carcanet, 2021), 270. Here, Dante is actually referring to his guide Beatrice Portinari—a Florentine woman with whom he was in

love in real life. His descriptions of Beatrice throughout *The Divine Comedy* often seem to be more fitting to Mary herself.

28   Lippi and Lucrezia: Only sparse and disputed details are known of Fra Lippi's relationship with the novice nun Lucrezia Buti, and these I have mostly gleaned from Vasari's *Lives of the Painters*. We know that Lippi "led away" the Dominican novice from a procession; we also know that the two (and possibly other religious) lived together afterward and that Lucrezia bore the painter two children. The couple were offered a papal dispensation to marry, but Lippi, a notorious letch, reportedly refused to take up the offer. In my account, the motives and emotions of those involved are surmised by me. Vasari claims that Lippi wanted to use Lucrezia as a model for the figure of the Madonna in his commissioned work for the chapel of Santa Margherita. Lippi may have painted more than one work for the nuns: a Nativity was reportedly plundered from the chapel during the Napoleonic wars. Another, *Madonna della Cintola*, has what seems to be the figure of Lucrezia Buti on the left-hand side of the painting as Saint Margherita. Lippi used Buti as a model for the Virgin Mary in many of his paintings, including *Madonna with Child and Two Angels*.

31   procession of the Girdle of St. Thomas: On Christmas, Easter, May 1, August 15, and September 8, the belt of the Virgin Mary is displayed in Prato, Italy. For the September feast, there is also a procession. The apocryphal story has it that St. Thomas witnessed Mary's Assumption to heaven, and she let down her belt to him as proof of what he had seen.

38   "the ancient Paradise was but a figure of her": Louis de Montfort, *True Devotion to Mary*, trans. William Frederick Faber (London: Catholic Way Publishing, 2013).

42   "woman must write her self": Hélène Cixous, "The Laugh of the Medusa," *Signs* 1, no. 4 (Summer 1976): 875–893.

42   if she wanted to say something it had better be brilliant and quick: I refer to Natalia Ginzburg's essay "Il Mio Mestiere" in *Le Piccole Virtù* (Torino: Einaudi, 2015).

43   "Write through the body": Cixous, "The Laugh of the Medusa."

43   "Have you seen him whom my soul loves?": Song of Solomon 3:3.

49   "None can sense more deeply than you artists": John Paul II, *Letter to Artists* 1, April 4, 1999, vatican.va.

58   made in the image and likeness: Genesis 1:26.

59   her Little Office: Books of Hours, which contained a version of *The Little Office of the Blessed Virgin Mary*, were in widespread use by religious and lay people alike through the Middle Ages. By the mid-fifteenth century, "the scholars at the newly founded Eton College said their Matins of the Virgin while making their beds" (Edmund Waterton, *Pietas Mariana Britannica* 1:31, quoted in Rachel Fulton Brown, *Mary and the Art of*

Prayer: The Hours of the Virgin in Medieval Christian Life and Thought (New York: Columbia University Press, 2018).

59   they sang those songs to her: Psalm 45 and 46, for example, are used as antiphons in *The Little Office of the Blessed Virgin Mary*, using the Gallican Psalter of St. Jerome, which refers to Jerusalem as "she" and in so doing evokes the city as a type of Mary.

59   "Before the ocean's depths were poured out": Proverbs 8:24, The Passion Translation. I use this translation because it specifically refers to "dancing" (as opposed to "brought forth," which is used in the NRSV-CE translation). The word translated as "brought forth" has overtones of "dancing" in the original Hebrew, and this encapsulates something joyful about sinlessness that we sometimes forget. Proverbs 8:30–31 also has echoes of David's dancing before the Lord in 2 Samuel 6:16.

60   "For she is a breath of the power of God": Wisdom 7:25–26.

60   "The doors, the doors!": From the Divine Liturgy of St. John Chrysostom.

60   "The Creator of our bodies knew what he was doing": St. Cyril of Jerusalem, *Catecheses* 9, 15, quoted in Thomas Spidlik, *Drinking from the Hidden Fountain: A Patristic Breviary* (New York: Cistercian, 1993).

61   "holy things for the holy": From the Divine Liturgy of St. John Chrysostom.

CHAPTER TWO: TOWER

67   "Again, one preparing to sail": Wisdom 14:1.

70   "Earth, divine goddess, Mother Nature": Twelfth-century English herbal, British Museum (MS. Harley, 1585, ff 12v-13r), quoted in Robert Graves, *The White Goddess* (London: Faber & Faber, 1948).

70   "who dost generate all things and bringest forth ever anew the sun": Graves, *The White Goddess.*

72   "The love of form is a love of endings": Louise Gluck, "Celestial Music," in *Ararat* (New York: Ecco, 2000).

75   "I must be myself": Ralph Waldo Emerson, "Self-Reliance," in *The Portable Emerson*, ed. Carl Bode and Malcolm Cowley (New York: Viking, 1981).

77   "I carried him who carries earth and sky": Frauenlob, *Marienleich*, strophes 11–13, trans. Barbara Newman, in *Frauenlob's Song of Songs*, 23–27, quoted in Rachel Fulton Brown, *Mary and the Art of Prayer: The Hours of the Virgin in Medieval Christian Life and Thought* (New York: Columbia University Press, 2018).

78   **"I am praise, I am majesty"**: The Pyramid Texts, in R.O. Faulkner, *The Ancient Egyptian Pyramid Texts* (Oxford: Clarendon, 1969), 181. Utterance 506 referenced in https://en.wikipedia.org/wiki/Bat_(goddess).

81   **deep and terrifying darkness**: Genesis 15:12.

86   **Abram built an altar**: Genesis 12:8.

86   **by the oaks he built another**: Genesis 13:18.

86   **Jacob built another**: Genesis 33:20.

87   **"The Lord is thy keeper"**: Psalm 121:5–6.

88   **"Am I not here who am your mother?"**: Words spoken by the Virgin Mary to the Mexican peasant Juan Diego in 1531 as he went to fetch a priest for his sick uncle. See "Our Lady of Guadalupe Resources," Xavier University website, accessed January 24, 2024, https://www.xavier.edu/jesuitresource/resources-by-theme/our-lady-of-guadalupe-resources.

89   **"For the first time in human history the mother kneels before her son"**: Simone de Beauvoir, *The Second Sex* (New York: Random House, 1997), 203.

89   **intent on becoming men**: In 2012, there were under 250 referrals to the Gender Identity Development Service in London, England, and most of them were male. In 2021, there were more than 5,000 referrals, two-thirds of which were adolescent girls experiencing gender dysphoria (Amelia Gentleman, "An Explosion: What Is Behind the Rise in Girls Questioning Their Gender Identity?" *The Guardian*, November 24, 2022, https://www.theguardian.com/society/2022/nov/24/an-explosion-what-is-behind-the-rise-in-girls-questioning-their-gender-identity).

90   **"My soul magnifies the Lord"**: Luke 1:46–55.

91   **she searched for him**: Luke 2:45.

91   **she stood at the window, asking for him**: Mark 3:32.

91   **she was at the wedding, telling him**: John 2:3.

91   **she waited under the cross**: John 19:25.

91   **"There must be something that lies outside of time in the bond between a mother and a child"**: Sofia Abasolo, Instagram post, "therealsofiaabasolo."

94   **"By his bruises we are healed"**: Isaiah 53:5.

98   **"One face looks out from all his canvases"**: Christina Rossetti, from her poem "In an Artist's Studio."

98   "spiritual transfiguration": Dante Gabriel Rossetti, in a letter of 1873, quoted at the Victorian Web, "Beata Beatrix," June 27, 2020, https://victorianweb.org/painting /dgr/paintings/6.html.

98   painted her in this transcendent pose: Gay Daly, *Pre-Raphaelites in Love* (New York: Ticknor & Fields, 1989), 93–94.

98–99   which Alighieri once dreamed that Beatrice ate: Dante Alighieri, *La Vita Nuova*, trans. Dante Gabriel Rossetti (London: Macmillan Collector's Library, 2021), 5.

100   "If the essence of everything I've ever said": Dante Alighieri, *Paradiso*, canto 30, from Ned Denny, *B (After Dante)* (Manchester: Carcanet, 2021), 317.

100   "She did not look like that, Monsieur": From the historical novel by Franz Werfel, *The Song of Bernadette*, trans. Ludwig Lewisohn (San Francisco: Ignatius, 2006), 451.

100   "If I had known that morning I would have to go sixty years": Roy Schoeman witness talk, December 15, 2022, Ludlow, Massachusetts, available at JewishCatholic, "Roy Schoeman Witness Talk December 15 Ludlow Massachusetts," YouTube video, January 17, 2023, https://youtu.be/CaBf8BRLB3o.

105   Queen of all hearts: Louis de Montfort, *True Devotion to Mary*, trans. William Frederick Faber (London: Catholic Way Publishing, 2013).

107   a self-help psychology book I'd bought on the subject: Lawrence J. Cohen, *The Opposite of Worry: The Playful Parenting Approach to Childhood Anxieties and Fears* (New York: Ballantine Books, 2013).

CHAPTER THREE: MOTHER

113   "spiritually a 'bitter sea' to the demons": Conrad of Saxony, *Speculum* III, ed. Pedro de Alcántara Martínez, trans. Sr. Mary Emmanuel, quoted in Rachel Fulton Brown, *Mary and the Art of Prayer: The Hours of the Virgin in Medieval Christian Life and Thought* (New York: Columbia University Press, 2018).

113   the strange story of the man across the fields at the base of the mountain: A similar incident is described in my poem "Mafia Flowers" (*Broken Sleep* [Northumberland, UK: Bloodaxe Books, 2008]). Such elaborate threats are typical of territories with criminal organizations or a vigilante element.

117   *Pro nois prega Maria*: A version of the *Regina Caeli* prayer in Sardinian.

118   *Odi et amo*: "I hate and I love," from Catullus 85.

120   "Christ stopped at Eboli": *Christ Stopped at Eboli* is a book by Carlo Levi, who was exiled to the Lucania region of Italy during the Second World War. The title comes

from a local expression, meaning that the area was bypassed by Christianity and, by extension, its civilizing influences and justice.

128   one of the visions experienced by St. Teresa of Avila: Recounted in *The Collected Works of Saint Teresa of Avila*, vol. 1, *The Book of her Life, Spiritual Testimonies and Soliloquies*, trans. Kieran Kavanaugh and Otilio Rodriguez (Washington, DC: ICS, 1987), 390–391.

129   "His mother treasured all these things in her heart": Luke 2:51.

131   "O you who dwell in the gardens": Song of Solomon 8:13.

143   "I slept with Thee till I grew pregnant with God's goodness": Frauenlob, *Marienleich*, strophes 11–13, trans. Barbara Newman, in *Frauenlob's Song of Songs*, 23–27, quoted in Fulton Brown, *Mary and the Art of Prayer*.

145   "handmaid of the Lord": Luke 1:38 NABRE.

145   "You will conceive in your womb": Luke 1:31.

145   it would be centuries before we understood: Marina Warner refers to these theories of Tertullian and Aristotle in her skeptical book *Alone of All Her Sex: The Myth and Cult of the Virgin Mary* (New York: Alfred A. Knopf, 1976). She goes on to say that the Church adopted the Aristotelian position through the work of Thomas Aquinas. Church teaching has since kept up with and endorsed scientific discovery about the biology of procreation.

149   "My soul magnifies the Lord": Luke 1:46–55.

153   drink to me with thine eyes: Referring to the first line of "To Celia" by Ben Jonson.

153   "Shall we be sundered?": A line of Celia's from William Shakespeare's *As You Like It*, act 1, scene 3.

154   "Alone of all your sex": A line from a poem by Caelius Sedulius, quoted and used as title by Marina Warner in *Alone of All Her Sex*.

157   "the heart's image": How Michelangelo described his *Pietà*, quoted in Tim McNeese, *Michelangelo: Painter, Sculptor and Architect* (New York: Chelsea House, 2005), 43.

158   "Help me, who am alone and have no helper but you": Esther 14:3.

158   "Why is light given to one in misery?": Job 3:20.

158   "My soul magnifies the Lord": Luke 1:46–55.

158 **"Each man kills the thing he loves"**: From "The Ballad of Reading Gaol" by Oscar Wilde, in *100 Great Catholic Poems*, ed. Sally Read (Elk Grove Village, IL: Word on Fire, 2023), 301.

159 **a novel will be published imagining that Mary *does* run away**: Colm Tóibín, *The Testament of Mary* (London: Penguin, 2013).

CHAPTER FOUR: THE ANSWERING CALL

165 **"And the Word became flesh"**: John 1:14.

167 **If anyone wants to take your coat, give your cloak as well**: See Matthew 5:40.

168 **"Who is my neighbor?"**: Luke 10:29.

169 **when I became Catholic**: The story of my conversion from atheism to the Catholic faith is told in my book *Night's Bright Darkness: A Modern Conversion Story* (San Francisco: Ignatius, 2016).

169 **"My Lord and my God"**: John 20:28.

169 **"There is no new revelation after Christ"**: "God has revealed himself fully by sending his own Son, in whom he has established his covenant forever. The Son is his Father's definitive Word; so there will be no further Revelation after him" (*Catechism of the Catholic Church* 73).

172 **Like everybody in the town, I knew the story**: The events of February 1995 in Civitavecchia, Italy, are well known in the area and are the subject of much documentation, reporting, and debate in the country, including by mainstream media. My recounting of these events is taken from Italian media and a book by Flavio Ubodi, vice-president of the Diocesan Theological Commission for the Madonnina of Civitavecchia, *La Madonna di Civitavecchia, Lacrime e Messaggi* (Milan: Edizioni Ares, 2018). Many devotees and pilgrims visit the statue in the Marian shrine of Sant'Agostino in Pantano, Civitavecchia, and many conversions and fruits are reported (see, for example, "A 'Weeping Image' of the Virgin, 10 Years On: Interview with Bishop Girolamo Grillo of Civitavecchia," February 10, 2005, Zenit, https://www.catholic.org/featured/headline.php?ID=1783). Other parties maintain that the weeping could have been pious fraud (see, for example, "The Crying Game," *The Guardian*, December 8, 2000, https://www.theguardian.com/theguardian/2000/dec/09/weekend7.weekend1). Whatever the truth of this little statue, it seems to me that the sheer quantity of reported Marian apparitions and messages throughout history and continuing to this day signal something important about our need for Mary.

173 **Kibeho**: Our Lady of Kibeho refers to a series of Marian apparitions in Rwanda in the 1980s. Mary is reported to have warned the seers of the upcoming genocide of 1994.

176   **it filled the coffin and it, with the fire, made the cemetery blaze:** Recounted in Gay Daly, *Pre-Raphaelites in Love* (Boston: Ticknor and Fields, 1989), 362–363.

176   **even a lock of her hair:** Locks of Sylvia Plath's hair are available for viewing in the Plath archive at the Lilly Library, Indiana University.

177   **said things that the uneducated Bernadette could never have dreamed up:** "I am the Immaculate Conception," Mary told Bernadette Soubirous in Lourdes, France, in 1858. The Immaculate Conception was a new dogma, and this vocabulary, particularly in this grammatical form, would not have been available to fourteen-year-old Bernadette, who struggled with her studies.

177   **"as one takes the hand of a child and guides it":** Franz Werfel, *The Song of Bernadette*, trans. Ludwig Lewisohn (San Francisco: Ignatius, 2006).

177   **to shepherd children of seven, nine, and ten:** In Fatima, Portugal, in 1917, Mary appeared six times to three shepherd children.

177   **to a fourteen-year-old and eleven-year-old in the Alps:** The apparition at La Salette.

177   **"I wish I could always weep like that":** The Desert Father was Abba Poemen (c. 340–450), quoted in *The Sayings of the Desert Fathers: The Alphabetical Collection*, trans. Benedicta Ward (Kalamazoo, MI: Cistercian, 1984), 187.

177   **La Salette:** In La Salette, France, in 1846, two children reported that a weeping lady spoke to them on a hillside. Due to the content of the lady's message, she was identified as Mary.

178   **consecration to Mary:** Louis de Montfort's eighteenth-century *True Devotion to Mary* contains a popular consecration to the Virgin. Written in poetic and, at times, hyperbolic language, it can be off-putting to those who do not understand its literary and theological context.

179   **"Do not gaze at me because I am dark":** Song of Solomon 1:6.

180   **"You shall know the truth and the truth shall make you odd":** Attributed to Flannery O'Connor.

180   **"Why have I found favor in your sight":** Ruth 2:10.

180   **"Do not be afraid, Mary, for you have found favor with God":** Luke 1:30.

181   **"If I should die, think only this of me":** From "The Soldier" by Rupert Brooke.

185   **even Jesus got left behind:** Luke 2:41–52.

185   **ὀδυνώμενοι, *odunomenoi*:** The Greek word for *anxiously*: "Look, your father and I have been searching for you in great anxiety" (Luke 2:48).

190 **"To fix one's thought on her is perfect understanding":** Wisdom 6:15.

193 **"We run to the odor of thy ointments":** Song of Solomon 1:3, quoted in *The Little Office of the Blessed Virgin Mary.*

196 ***Sub tuum praesidium confugimus, sancta dei genitrix:*** "We fly to thy protection, O holy Mother of God" in Latin.

198 **"My God, my God, why have you forsaken me?":** Matthew 27:46.

198 **"The abandonment at the supreme moment of the crucifixion":** Simone Weil, *Gravity and Grace* (Oxford: Routledge, 2002), 87.

201 **"Min dryhten God Aelmihtig":** "My Lord God Almighty" in Old English.

201 ***Domine, labia mea aperies:*** "Lord, open my lips," from Psalm 51 in Latin.

204 **"All that seek me there shall find succor":** From "The Pynson Ballad," printed in 1485 by Robert Pynson.

204 **"So neither the one who plants nor the one who waters":** 1 Corinthians 3:7.

204 **"Unless the Lord builds the house":** Psalm 127:1.

204 **"You are God's field, God's building":** 1 Corinthians 3:9.

204 **"I am the field that bore in season":** Frauenlob, *Marienleich*, strophes 11–13, trans. Barbara Newman, in *Frauenlob's Song of Songs*, 23–27, quoted in Rachel Fulton Brown, *Mary and the Art of Prayer: The Hours of the Virgin in Medieval Christian Life and Thought* (New York: Columbia University Press, 2018).

205 **a woman of the thin place:** "The thin place" is, of course, Walsingham, and any place that God uses Mary to thin the veil between heaven and earth. For this account of the Walsingham story, I've taken historian Bill Flint's theory that "Richeldis," visionary of Walsingham, was Edith the Fair, wife of the last Anglo-Saxon King of England, Harold Godwinson (see *Edith the Fair: Visionary of Walsingham* [Leominster, UK: Gracewing Publishing, 2015]). "Richeldis" is a nickname meaning "rich and fair." The circumstances of the vision told here are invented by me, particularly the illness of Godwin, the eldest son. It is fair, however, to assume that Edith went through the anxiety of illness, and even bereavement, common to parents of that time. We also know of the ongoing battles with which her husband was involved and that he is said to have been miraculously cured of paralysis as a child (in gratitude for which he would later build Waltham Abbey). For the facts of the visions, most of our knowledge comes from the fifteenth-century "Pynson Ballad": that in 1061 the Lady of Walsingham Manor (Edith the Fair) petitioned Our Lady to show her a way to honor her, and the Virgin took her in spirit to the house of Nazareth three times. She then asked Richeldis to build a copy of that house in Walsingham. In the morning, two shapes were dry on the dewy grass outside. Richeldis asked workmen to build on one of them, but the building didn't go well. During the night the house was miraculously constructed on the other

patch of dry land. In time, Walsingham became a busy pilgrimage destination—the most popular Christian site after Santiago de Compostela and Jerusalem. Edith fled to the very north of Europe sometime after the Norman conquest of 1066. The house and shrine were torn down during the Reformation but were rebuilt by the Anglican church in the 1930s, albeit on a different spot in the village. A Catholic shrine was completed outside the village in 1982, near to the Slipper Chapel, which was originally built in 1340 as a last stop on the pilgrimage to Walsingham. My impression of the Walsingham vision is greatly influenced by convert Roy Schoeman's account of his dream of the Virgin, recounted in JewishCatholic, "Roy Schoeman Witness Talk December 15 Ludlow Massachusetts," YouTube video, January 17, 2023, https://youtu.be/CaBf8BRLB30.

206 **"Woman clothed with the sun":** Revelation 12:1.

212 **Some say that this Madonna was actually saved:** Fr. Michael Rear and Dr. Francis Young discuss the likelihood of the Langham Madonna being the original Lady of Walsingham statue in "Was the original Walsingham statue really destroyed—or is it in the V&A?," *The Catholic Herald*, July 25, 2019, https://catholicherald.co.uk/was-the -original-walsingham-statue-really-destroyed-or-is-it-in-the-va/.

214 *La soberana doctora de la escuelas divinas*: "The sovereign doctor of the divine schools," from Carol 219 by Sor Juana Inés de la Cruz.

214 **"But look upon the lovely face":** Dante Alighieri, *Paradiso*, canto 32, from Ned Denny, B *(After Dante)* (Manchester: Carcanet, 2021), 325.

215 **"And from that hour the disciple took her into his own home":** John 19:27. I am indebted to Pope Benedict XVI for his writing on Mary, particularly his exegesis of this verse (General Audience, August 12, 2009, vatican.va) and his elucidation of the grounds for believing that the Virgin should be identified with Wisdom of the Old Testament. And—the decisive Marian image for me—that "there is a pure answer and . . . God's love finds an irrevocable dwelling place within it" (Joseph Ratzinger, *Daughter Zion: Meditations on the Church's Marian Belief*, trans. John M. McDermott [San Francisco: Ignatius, 1985], 26).

216–217 **list of Marian titles:** These Marian titles are taken from the litanies of Loreto, Sorrows, and Carmel, with "Key of Heaven, Scripture's Comment and Gloss, Medicine Chest of God, Cell of the Word, Abyss of Honey, Casket of Celestial Incense, Saw of Death" from "Ave Virgo Mater Christi" by Walter of Wimborne; "Air We Breathe, Wondrous Robe, Wild Web" from Gerard Manley Hopkins' "The Blessed Virgin compared to the Air we Breathe"; and "Pane of Glass" referring to Thomas Merton's poem "The Blessed Virgin Mary Compared to a Window." Other titles of Mary are taken from various apparitions and devotions; "lamp by the bedside" and the last seven are my own invented titles.

Works of Art

Ophelia. John Everett Millais, 1851–1852 (Tate Britain, London, England).

Proserpine. Dante Gabriel Rossetti, 1874 (Tate Britain, London, England).

The Virgin of the Rocks. Leonardo da Vinci, 1506–1508 (National Gallery, London, England).

The Holy Virgin Mary. Chris Ofili, 1996 (Museum of Modern Art, New York, USA).

Madonna and Child and an Angel. Hans Baldung Grien, 1539 (Barnes, Philadelphia, USA).

Madonna. Edvard Munch, 1892–1895 (Munch Museum, Oslo, Norway).

Madonna of the Pinks. Raphael, 1506–1507 (National Gallery, London, England).

CHAPTER TWO

The Madonna of the Prairie. William Henry Dethlef Koerner, 1922 (Buffalo Bill Center of the West, Wyoming, USA).

Madonna and Child. Alfreda Beartrack (Aktà Lakota Museum and Cultural Center, St. Joseph's Indian School, Chamberlain, South Dakota, USA).

Madonna of Guadalupe. Acheiropoieton, 1531 (Basilica of Our Lady of Guadalupe, Mexico City, Mexico).

The Virgin and Child with Saint Anne and the Infant John the Baptist ("The Burlington House Cartoon"). Leonardo da Vinci, 1499–1500 (National Gallery, London, England).

Beata Beatrix. Dante Gabriel Rossetti, 1870 (Tate Britain, London, England).

The Annunciation. John William Waterhouse, 1914 (private collection).

The Annunciation. Edward Burne-Jones, 1879 (Lady Lever Art Gallery, Liverpool, England).

The Annunciation. Dante Gabriel Rossetti, 1855 (Agnew's, London, England).

The Annunciation. Dante Gabriel Rossetti, 1861 (Fitzwilliam Museum, Cambridge, England).

Ecce Ancilla Domini. Dante Gabriel Rossetti, 1849–1850 (Tate Britain, London, England).

CHAPTER THREE

Madonna of the Rose Bower. Stefan Lochner, 1440–1442 (Richartz Museum, Cologne, Germany).

Sheeted Madonna. Unknown. (I haven't been able to trace the framed picture of the Virgin given to me by Liz.)

The Annunciation. Caravaggio, 1608 (Musée de Beaux-Arts de Nancy, France).

The Annunciation. Filippo Lippi, 1450–1453 (National Gallery, London, England).

The Annunciation. Sandro Botticelli, 1489–1490 (Uffizzi Gallery, Florence, Italy).

The Annunciation. Guido Reni, 1629 (Louvre, Paris, France).

The Annunciation. Leonardo da Vinci, c. 1472 (Uffizzi Gallery, Florence, Italy).

The Annunciation. John William Waterhouse, 1914 (private collection).

The Annunciation. Carlo Crivelli, 1486 (National Gallery, London, England).

The Annunciation. Henry Ossawa Tanner, 1898 (Philadelphia Museum of Art, Philadelphia, USA).

The Annunciation. Fra Angelico, 1440–1445 (Convent of San Marco, Florence, Italy).

The Annunciation. Salomon Koninck, 1655 (Hallwyl Museum, Stockholm, Sweden).

The Annunciation. John Collier, 2000 (Church of Saint Gabriel, McKinney, Texas, USA).

La Madonna del Parto. Piero della Francesca, 1460 (Musei Civici, Monterchi, Tuscany, Italy).

La Pietà. Michelangelo, 1498–1499 (Saint Peter's Basilica, Rome, Italy).

Photographs by Robert Hupka of the *Pietà*, 1964–1965.

CHAPTER FOUR

Reverse Graffiti. William Kentridge, 2016 (the walls of Rome, Italy).

Madonna dei Pellegrini. Caravaggio, 1604–1606 (Basilica of Saint Augustine, Rome, Italy).

Salus Populi Romani. Luke the Evangelist, c. 85 (Basilica of Saint Mary Major, Rome, Italy).

La Madonna della Strada. Thirteenth–fourteenth century (Church of the Gesù, Rome, Italy).

The Madonna Uniting Saint Catherine of Alexandria in Mystical Union with the Christ Child. Anonymous, entitled by the author, sixteenth century (private collection).

La Madonna del Granduca. Raphael, 1506–1507 (Uffizi Gallery, Florence, Italy).

Edith Finding the Body of Harold on the Battlefield of Hastings. Charles Augustus William Wilke, 1875 (West Marina Gardens, Hastings, England).

The Statue of Our Lady of Walsingham. Walsingham, England. Some theorize that the original statue (the thirteenth-century Langham Madonna) was saved during the Reformation and is currently housed in the Victoria and Albert Museum, London, England.

Bibliography

Beauvoir, Simone de. *The Second Sex*. Edited by Ruth Evans. Manchester: Manchester University Press, 2013.

Cixous, Hélène. "The Laugh of the Medusa." Translated by Keith Cohen and Paula Cohen. *Signs* 1, no. 4 (Summer 1976): 875–893.

Daly, Gay. *Pre-Raphaelites in Love*. Boston: Ticknor and Fields, 1989.

de Montfort, Louis. *True Devotion to Mary*. Translated by William Frederick Faber. London: Catholic Way Publishing, 2013.

Flint, Bill. *Edith the Fair: Visionary of Walsingham*. Leominster, UK: Gracewing Publishing, 2015.

Fulton Brown, Rachel. *Mary and the Art of Prayer: The Hours of the Virgin in Medieval Christian Life and Thought*. New York: Columbia University Press, 2018.

Graves, Robert. *The White Goddess*. London: Faber and Faber, 1948.

The Little Office of the Blessed Virgin Mary. London: Baronius, 2020.

Pynson, Richard. "The Pynson Ballad." England, ca. 1485.

Ratzinger, Joseph. *Daughter Zion: Meditations on the Church's Marian Belief.* Translated by John M. McDermott. San Francisco: Ignatius, 1985.

Ubodi, Flavio. *La Madonna di Civitavecchia, Lacrime e Messaggi.* Milano: Edizioni Ares, 2018.

Vasari, Giorgio. *The Lives of the Most Excellent Painters, Sculptors and Architects.* Florence: Giunti, 1568.

Warner, Marina. *Alone of All Her Sex: The Myth and Cult of the Virgin Mary.* New York: Alfred A. Knopf, 1976.